Franklin D. Roosevelt

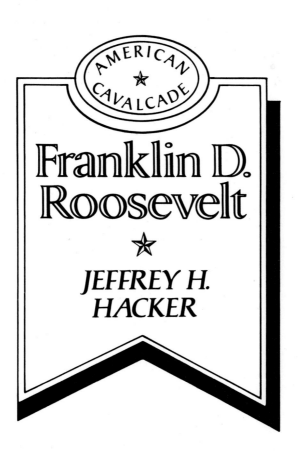

AMERICAN CAVALCADE

Franklin D. Roosevelt

★

JEFFREY H. HACKER

MARSHALL CAVENDISH
CORPORATION

GREY CASTLE PRESS

Published by Grey Castle Press, Lakeville, Connecticut.

Marshall Cavendish Edition, North Bellmore, New York.

Published in large print by arrangement with Franklin Watts, Inc.

Printed in the USA.

Library of Congress Cataloging-in-Publication Data

Hacker, Jeffrey H.
    Franklin D. Roosevelt / by Jeffrey H. Hacker.
        p.   cm. — (American cavalcade)
    Reprint. Originally published : New York : F. Watts, 1983.
    Includes bibliographical references and index.
    Summary: A biography of the man who was elected to the presidency four times and provided inspired leadership during the Depression and, later, in the face of the Nazi menace.
    ISBN 1-55905-096-9 (Grey Castle : lg. print)
    1. Roosevelt, Franklin D. (Franklin Delano), 1882–1945—Juvenile literature.   2. United States—Politics and government—1933–1945—Juvenile literature.   3. Presidents— United States—Biography—Juvenile literature.   4. Large type books.   [1. Roosevelt, Franklin D. (Franklin Delano), 1882–1945.   2. Presidents.   3. Large type books.]
    I. Title.   II. Series.
    [E807.H28 1991]
    973.917′092—dc20
    [B]
    [92]   90-48973
                                                                                                    CIP
                                                                                                    AC

ISBN 1-55905-096-9
        1-55905-100-0 (set)

Photo Credits:

Cover: Franklin D. Roosevelt Library
Franklin D. Roosevelt Library—pgs. 17, 25, 29, 35, 40, 51, 63
U.S. Army Signal Corps—pgs. 126, 148

Keystone Underwood—pg. 70
U.P.I.—pg. 80
Yank—pg. 154
Tenschert/Capitol Photo Archives—pg. 159

Contents

A Day of Consecration

ON INAUGURATION DAY, 1929, President Herbert Hoover could declare with confidence that ''we in America today are nearer to the final triumph over poverty than ever before in the history of any land.'' The decade of the 1920s was one of unbounded prosperity and optimism. The stock market, fueled by speculation and credit buying, climbed ever upward. Short skirts and bobbed hair, roadsters, rumble seats, and raccoon coats symbolized a spirit of carefree exuberance. The automobile, radio, and motion pictures were popular new diversions that brought major changes to the American way of life. Jazz set the rhythm. The future looked bright.

Then the bottom fell out. The stock market crash of October 1929 marked the end of the Jazz Age and the beginning of the darkest, most severe Depression in the nation's history. Businesses failed by the thousands. Industrial and farm production dropped precipitously. Unemployment jumped to 4 million in 1930, 8 million in 1931, and 12 million in 1932. Property owners who couldn't meet their mortgage payments lost their homes. Banks closed down as panicky customers withdrew their money. The jobless roamed the country, living as hoboes or in ''Hoovervilles''— clusters of shabby tin huts. Breadlines stretched for blocks. Once-prosperous businessmen sold apples on street corners. The system had failed. Some talked of revolution.

By Inauguration Day, 1933, the United States was facing its bleakest moment since the Civil War. On that Saturday, March 4, a chill drizzle fell from dreary skies over the nation's capital. By noon every bank in the country had been forced to shut down. More than 13 million Americans— about one-fourth of the work force—were out of jobs. Herbert Hoover, the outgoing president, could now only admit: ''We are at the end of our string.''

The president-elect in March 1933 was a 51-year-old former governor of New York with a flair for the dramatic. The previous July he had flown to Chicago to accept the Democratic nomination, the first time a winning candidate had ever gone before the party convention. His legs withered by polio, Franklin Delano Roosevelt conducted a vigorous campaign, promising "a new deal for the American people." Though he won by a landslide, Roosevelt knew that his election reflected a demand for change rather than any real confidence in his own leadership. The respected journalist Walter Lippmann had described Roosevelt as "a pleasant man who, without any important qualifications for the office, would very much like to be President." Heywood Broun, another noted columnist, saw him as "the corkscrew candidate of a convoluting convention."

Now at the inaugural, a crowd of 100,000 huddled before the Capitol rotunda. The rest of America, demoralized and yearning for hope, listened to radio sets. Franklin Roosevelt stood on the platform, his weight supported by steel leg braces, his chin thrust forward. Chief Justice Charles Evans Hughes administered the oath of office, Roosevelt repeating each phrase in a cold, ringing pitch. A stiff wind rippled the pages of his speech as the new president turned to the cheerless crowd.

"This is a day of national consecration," he began. "I am certain that my fellow Americans expect that on my induction into the presidency I will address them with a candor and a decision which the present situation of our nation impels. This is preeminently the time to speak the truth, the whole truth, frankly and boldly. Nor need we shrink from honestly facing conditions in our country today. This great nation will endure as it has endured, will revive and will prosper.

"So first of all," he continued, "let me assert my firm belief that the only thing we have to fear is fear itself—nameless, unreasoning, unjustified terror which paralyzes needed efforts to convert retreat into advance. . . . This nation asks for action, and action now."

The 1933 inaugural address was one of the few times Franklin Roosevelt would deliver a speech under cloudy skies. Political opponents, exasperated as much by his sheer good fortune as by his popularity, coined the term "Roosevelt weather" for the sometimes miraculous way the skies cleared when FDR was scheduled to speak. "Happy days are here again/The skies above are clear again," went his song.

Making good on his promise for action, the new president quickly instituted a series of measures to reopen the banks and reverse the slide toward complete economic and social disaster. His air of confidence and boldness of action stirred hope. His charismatic presence—the toss of his head, big smile, and jaunty self-assurance—sparked a renewal of spirit. His personal courage in overcoming a crippling disease further inspired a downtrodden people. America had not really known what to expect, but now there was a glimmer of light. Walter Lippmann was among the millions who were quickly won over. "In one week," he wrote, "the nation, which had lost confidence in everything and everybody, has regained confidence in the government and itself." Franklin Roosevelt had indeed given the American people a "new deal."

If the Great Depression was the most dangerous domestic crisis faced by the United States in the twentieth century, certainly the greatest foreign menace was posed by Adolf Hitler. Again, Franklin Roosevelt was there to inspire the nation, calm and reassure it through hard times, and lead it to its greatest victory. The United States emerged from World War II with a new sense of its own worth and a new respect on the world scene.

By mere virtue of his leadership during the two most critical moments in modern American history, Franklin Roosevelt must rank as one of the nation's great presidents. He was elected to the office four times—1932, 1936, 1940, and 1944—more than any other president past or future. (The Twenty-second Amendment to the U.S. Constitution, adopted in 1951, established two terms as the maximum for any president.) Roosevelt held the office for more than twelve years, using his power to make government more responsive to, and more responsible for, the well-being of the people. For those twelve years, he *was* the presidency, and it was hard to imagine anyone else in the White House. The story is told of a farmer displaying his newborn son to a neighbor. "Perhaps he'll grow up to be president," said the neighbor. "What's wrong with Mr. Roosevelt?" shot back the farmer. Many who survived the Depression looked upon FDR as their personal savior. Historians and political scholars rank him as one of America's great leaders.

Despite these legitimate claims to greatness and despite the wild adoration of millions of Americans, Franklin Roosevelt was also one of our most controversial presidents. For as deeply as some loved the man, others hated him. The qualities that so many admired, others detested. What some called strength of character and confidence of conviction, others regarded as stubbornness and arrogance. The good humor and cheerful optimism that endeared him to citizens in all walks of life were viewed by his critics as evasion, blithe indifference, or just plain deceitfulness. He was "Mr. Roosevelt" to those who loved him, "That Man in the White House" to his detractors.

Nearly four decades after Roosevelt's passing, the debate goes on. Certainly the hope and inspiration he brought to the American people were supremely important during times of trouble. Certainly there was no failure of nerve or leadership in the face of the Great Depression or the Nazi menace. And without question, Roosevelt was a passionate defender of equal opportunity and democratic government. Nevertheless, an objective look at his record shows that there were also failures, oversights, hesitations, deceptions, political manipulations, and blatant attempts to expand presidential power. All was not greatness.

To begin with, Roosevelt's New Deal did not really end the Depression. As of 1941, there were still several million Americans looking for jobs that did not exist. Only with the outbreak of World War II and a vast expansion of the arms industry did mass unemployment really disappear and the economy really recover. Moreover, the New Deal did not represent a cohesive, carefully planned program. The uncertainty of it all was summed up by Eleanor Roosevelt at the time of her husband's inauguration. "One has a tremendous feeling of it going blindly," she wrote, "because we're in a tremendous stream, and none of us knows where we're going to land."

Several of the most important New Deal initiatives landed in the Supreme Court, where they were declared unconstitutional. To get back at the justices, Roosevelt presented a plan in 1937 that became known as the "court-packing scheme." According to the proposal, the president would be allowed to appoint several additional justices, thereby making the body more favorable to his own ideas. The scheme aroused fierce controversy and, after months of debate, was overwhelmingly rejected by the Senate. It was the deepest humiliation of FDR's political life.

Despite the successful outcome of World War II, Roosevelt has also been criticized for a variety of mistakes and injustices during the war years: that he was ill prepared for the attack on Pearl Harbor; that his imprisonment of Japanese-Americans was an unwarranted violation of their civil liberties; that he was unsympathetic to the plight of European Jews; and that his shortsighted diplomacy planted the seeds of the Cold War.

Long after his death in 1945, researchers discovered other unflattering details of Roosevelt's public and private lives. First it was revealed that Franklin had had a secret love affair with a young woman named Lucy Mercer, Eleanor's social secretary. Then, in 1982, it was disclosed that Roosevelt had bugged the Oval Office in the months prior to the 1940 presidential election; the recordings include discussions between Roosevelt and political aides on ways to smear the character of Republican candidate Wendell Willkie.

FDR was a man of contradiction and controversy. He was confident; he was unsure of himself. He was innovative; he was old-fashioned. He had a flair for the dramatic; he wallowed in hesitation. Proud and humble, he stuck to his guns but was open to new ideas. He was both pragmatic and idealistic. He was warm and personable, yet few knew him well. Harold Ickes, for years a close adviser, wrote in his diary: "I cannot come to grips with him." Clearly a statesman of stature, Franklin Roosevelt was perhaps our most ambiguous and most mystifying president. His "day of national consecration" was in reality a day of uncertainty, in his own mind as well as in the minds of the people. In many ways FDR is still an uncertainty.

Perhaps he wanted it that way. A master politician, Roosevelt recognized the need to adapt and change. He espoused no firm ideology, except what was practical and expedient, and was anxious to try new ideas when old ones failed. His most severe criticism of any proposal was: "That all sounds very theoretical to me." By remaining uncommitted to any particular interest group or way of thinking, he could remain flexible, both as a leader and as a politician. His victories on election day were largely attributable to that flexibility. Mystification was both a strategy and a byproduct of his political style. No one knew everything he was doing or why he was doing it. That way he couldn't be trapped.

Attacking the Roosevelt style, Herbert Hoover in the 1932 campaign called his opponent a ''chameleon.'' It was a label that FDR's critics would apply again and again over the next twelve years. The implication was that he tried to be all things to all people, blending in with the changing landscape of political opinion. More dispassionately, one major biographer, James MacGregor Burns, described him as part lion, part fox. Another important historian, Arthur Schlesinger, Jr., agreed. ''He could roar like the lion,'' said Schlesinger, ''and dissemble like the fox.'' He showed strength and courage; he was sly and scheming. He struck fear in his enemies; he cleverly outsmarted them.

But those descriptions are also incomplete. Beyond chameleon, beyond lion, and beyond fox, Roosevelt is also remembered as the Great Communicator. Without bluster and without doubletalk, he addressed the people simply and directly. In his famous Fireside Chats (radio talks), he explained complicated issues in clear, no-nonsense terms. He was the first president to hold open press conferences with spontaneous answers to

The first "media president," Roosevelt used his famous Fire-side Chats (radio talks) to explain government policies and boost the morale of the people.

unseen questions. In short, his presidency marked the beginning of "media politics" in America.

Talking to the people in their living rooms had political advantages, and Roosevelt had more than his share of battles with the press. But no matter how he communicated and how he conducted his political wars, his single most important goal was the general welfare of the people. As lion and as fox, FDR's motivating principle was that government had a responsibility to do everything in its power to preserve the freedoms—political, social, and economic—of every citizen. He regarded that as a deep moral obligation, with the result that many of his speeches sounded like sermons. Whatever his tactics—power, guile, or sermonizing—his ultimate purpose was to defend and promote the democratic freedoms of the people.

Today Franklin Roosevelt is often blamed for the excessive role of the federal government in everyday American life, for the excessive power of organized labor, and for the excessive authority of the president. But whether or not all three areas have grown to excess, and whether or not Roosevelt is to blame, the thirty-second president of the United States can be credited with having begun a new and lasting trend in national government: to provide more for the greatest number of people.

In weighing the pluses and minuses of the Roosevelt presidency, one inevitably has to consider the costs and consequences of that trend.

But whether one is a liberal or a conservative, a Democrat or a Republican, there is no disputing the fact that FDR has had a greater impact on the American scene than any other twentieth-century president. In economic and social policy, in foreign affairs, and in the political process itself, the Age of Roosevelt set precedents and established directions with which every subsequent president has had to contend. Since FDR, the American public has come to expect greatness from its leaders. For many, Roosevelt is the standard by which presidents are to be measured. His legacy to the nation—indeed to the world—is as tangible as the Grand Coulee Dam, as certain as the defeat of Hitler, and as controversial as the welfare state.

The lasting picture of Franklin Roosevelt is of a crippled but energetic president posing behind the wheel of a campaign touring car. The chin is thrust forward, and the cigarette holder is at a jaunty tilt. Blue eyes twinkle behind rimless glasses, and the smile is wide.

The story of Franklin Roosevelt is of a child born into patrician wealth who grew up to be a champion of the "forgotten" poor. It is the story of a man whom many credit as their savior, but whom some call villain. In either case, it is the story of an important life in tumultuous times.

2

Soil and Roots

*"All that is in me
goes back to the Hudson."*

THE ROOSEVELT ESTATE at Hyde Park, New York, is a
vast expanse of woods, gardens, and sloping
lawns overlooking the Hudson River from an eastern perch. The family residence in 1882 was an
airy clapboard house with shutters on every win-
dow and a narrow veranda framed in ivy. The
house had been purchased twenty-five years before by James Roosevelt, an enterprising busi-
nessman and country squire.

James was a seventh-generation Roosevelt, the
descendant of a Dutch settler of the 1640s. The
family tree had two main branches, one originat-
ing with Jacobus Roosevelt (James' great-great-
grandfather) and the other with Jacobus' brother,
Johannes. The two lines are significant in that
each one produced a president of the United
States—Theodore Roosevelt from the Johannes

line and Franklin D. Roosevelt from the Jacobus line. The Jacobus branch of the family included only one other politician, and he during the period of the American Revolution. Subsequent generations led quieter provincial lives in upstate New York. English, German, and other strains entered the bloodline as the generations passed.

James Roosevelt was of mainly Anglo-Saxon inheritance. A tall, slender man with muttonchop side-whiskers, he carried himself with a quiet and gentle dignity that won respect in business circles and admiration in the Hudson River Valley. He was graduated from Union College in 1847 and, except for one brief adventure, moved steadily into the life of a business executive and country gentleman. On a walking tour of Italy in 1848, he enlisted in the nationalist army of Giuseppe Garibaldi and participated in a siege of Naples. After just two months, he resumed his tour and then returned to the States. Graduating from Harvard Law School in 1851, he took over the family investments in coal and transportation, becoming a vice-president of one large company and the head of several smaller ones. Seeking greater financial power, he made large investments in coal and railroads, but these proved unsuccessful. Still wealthy, he retired to a life of leisure at Hyde Park with his wife, Rebecca, and their son, James (Rosy) Roosevelt. When Rebecca died in 1876, the elder James was 48.

For the country gentleman widower, life was to begin again four years later, when, at the New York City home of Theodore Roosevelt, he was introduced to a distant cousin named Sara (Sallie) Delano. Sara was 26 years old, the same age as his son, Rosy, and exactly half his own age. Her father, Warren Delano, had known James through business. Though he admired Roosevelt, Delano resisted the match because of the great difference in age. Despite his protests, the couple was married in October 1880. After an extended honeymoon abroad, James and Sara Roosevelt settled at Hyde Park.

Their life was tranquil and happy. James did little business, spending most of his time hunting, raising livestock, traveling, and serving in various community organizations. Sara cared for her husband with great affection and thrived in her role as mistress of the estate. They lived in genteel luxury, with a complete staff of servants: maids, governesses, cooks, coachmen, gardeners, and farmhands. It was old-family wealth, and they believed in the old-fashioned standard of *noblesse oblige*—that members of the upper class have an obligation to be honorable, generous, and responsible citizens.

It was into this world that Franklin Delano Roosevelt was born. On the evening of January 30, 1882, James Roosevelt made the following entry in his wife's diary: "At a quarter to nine my Sallie had a splendid large baby boy. He weighs 10 lbs., without clothes." Sara later described her infant son as "plump, pink, and nice."

Franklin would lose his plumpness, becoming in fact rather thin and spindly. But, according to his mother, he was always "a good little boy." His childhood was happy and secure, though somewhat isolated from the world outside. Rosy was grown up, and there were no other children to compete for attention. Franklin was doted on by his parents, servants, aunts, and uncles. And though life at Hyde Park revolved around the child, he was carefully sheltered from any quarrel or unpleasantness. His parents kept him in dresses and long blond curls until he was 5. For several years more he wore kilts and Little Lord Fauntleroy suits.

Franklin's upbringing was more that of a country gentleman than a president of the United States. James and Sara felt that a career in politics would be beneath his social standing, and Sara later told him so. But whatever their wishes, the Roosevelts instilled in their son many values and personal qualities that would bring success in the political arena—high-mindedness, an old-fashioned sense of duty, and a feeling of responsibility for the less fortunate.

Two important ingredients in the development of Franklin's character were his sheltered upbringing and his isolation from children his own age. Eleanor Roosevelt later described a tendency which likely was the result of overprotection. "If something was unpleasant and he didn't want to know about it," she said, "he just ignored it and never talked about it. He always thought that if you ignored a thing long enough it would settle itself."

Franklin did have playmates from neighboring estates—the Rogers boys and Mary Newbold—but he spent a great deal of his time in the company of adults. His parents participated in many of his activities at Hyde Park, and summers he traveled with them to Europe, the New England shore, or the family cottage at Campobello Island off the coast of New Brunswick, Canada. He was never without a governess, and he was schooled by private tutors until age 14. One result was a strong loyalty to his family and an abiding commitment to their social standards. Another consequence, at least according to some biographers, was that being popular became extremely important later in life. Finally, to get what he wanted

The Roosevelt estate at Hyde Park, NY, was the family home long before Franklin was born. The future president enjoyed an idyllic youth on its vast grounds and returned to it often throughout his life to think and rest.

from the adults around him, young Franklin learned that charm and good manners were more persuasive than crying or stamping his feet.

There were, to be sure, very few things the boy wanted that he did not get. He had his own pony by the time his legs were long enough to ride and several dogs. His father gave him his first gun and taught him to shoot at age 11. And when he wanted to learn to sail, James hired a sea captain to teach the young squire, gave Franklin the use of his yacht, the *Half Moon*, and eventually bought him his own 21-footer, the *New Moon*. Young Franklin tended his own garden and built tree houses in the woods. He iceboated on the river, walked in the fields, and gradually learned every tree and rock on the estate. He loved the outdoors and grew up with an appreciation of the delicate balances of nature. As a public official, he would give special emphasis to conservation and land renewal programs. "The forests," he once said, "are the lungs of our land, purifying our air and giving fresh strength to our people."

Collecting things—birds, stamps, model ships, and anything to do with the Navy—was another boyhood passion. He shot and stuffed as many different birds as he could find at Hyde Park, building a remarkably complete collection of Dutchess County specimens. He got interested in stamps and, with the addition of several albums given to him by an uncle, put together a collection that eventually became world famous. Finally, he treasured any book, model, or picture pertaining to the U.S. Navy. Collecting and sailing were two childhood hobbies that Franklin would turn to throughout his life.

"All that is in me goes back to the Hudson," said Roosevelt many years later. His family had lived on its banks for generations. Hyde Park was where Franklin was born and where he would be buried. It was where his character—everything from his sense of right and wrong to his love of ships—had begun to take shape. It was where he took his fiancée on long walks. It was his base of operations as a young politician. And when he was president, it was where he would go to think and renew his strength. Hyde Park was home soil, and he would always return to it.

Groton

Sara had taken an active interest in her son's education, carefully supervising a succession of governesses and tutors. The boy was drilled in German, French, Latin, mathematics, history, and penmanship, with his mother closely monitoring his daily progress. Sara and James kept him at home as long as they could but realized that sooner or later he would have to go off to school. Finally they made plans to enroll him in a small prep school for boys in Groton, Massachusetts, 50 miles outside Boston. The founder and headmaster, the Reverend Endicott Peabody, preferred that all boys attend for the full six-year period, but Franklin was accepted for the Third Form. In September 1896 James and Sara left their shy 14-year-old in the hands of Reverend Peabody. "It is hard to leave our darling boy," Sara wrote in her diary. "James and I feel this parting very much."

Groton School was modeled after the great schools of England, such as Eton and Harrow, where the privileged class sent its sons for moral, social, and intellectual training. The avowed goal of Reverend Peabody was to cultivate in each of his 110 students "manly Christian character." For young Franklin, it was a potentially difficult adjustment. At Hyde Park he had been doted on, overprotected, and most often in the company of adults. Now he was just one of many students. He lived in a small, spartan cubicle and had to take care of himself. His classmates had all been together for two years, and in a social environment in which being popular was extremely important, Franklin was the "new kid." Athletics was the single most important activity at Groton, but Roosevelt was slight of build and did not excel at sports.

Despite these adversities, Franklin made a relatively smooth transition. "I am getting on fine both mentally and physically," he wrote his parents. While he never achieved the grand popularity he hoped for, neither was he the object of the sometimes cruel pranks played by older students. He learned to conform to the rules and social standards of school life, and he took part in many activities. He played intramural football, was a member of the debating team, sang in the choir, and was manager of the baseball team. In his second year he won the Punctuality Prize, but he also took a few black marks to show the other students that he had "school spirit." Academ-

Home from the Groton School at age 17, Franklin poses with father James and mother Sara Delano Roosevelt. Strong-minded Sara was James' second wife; Franklin was her only child.

ically, his record was undistinguished—a ''C'' average in his first semesters, barely moving up to a ''B.''

Franklin has at least two nicknames in prep school, one of which was ''Uncle Frank.'' Teddy Roosevelt—the son of his half-brother, Rosy—was a year ahead of him at Groton, and the oddity of having an older nephew did not escape the other students. Some schoolmates, finding him a bit superficial and a lightweight socially, took to calling him ''feather duster.'' During his four years at Groton, Franklin did grow modestly in self-assurance and popularity. He was greatly disappointed at not being named a senior prefect, and he was still thin and gangly. But several students came to like and admire him. He was remembered by one as ''cool and self-possessed,'' with a ''friendly and understanding smile.'' Dr. Peabody later described him as ''a quiet, satisfactory boy.''

The Reverend Peabody had a lasting effect on Roosevelt's life. The rector was a strict disciplinarian who demanded absolute obedience to God and Country. Conservative and puritanical, he defended the established social order and preached old-fashioned Christian morality. To preserve the status quo, he urged his boys to make careers in politics and public service. Preparation for political leadership was, he felt, essential to the development of manly Christian character. For the upper class, serving society was a Christian duty. And while the curriculum at Groton did not give much useful background in history or politics, few students would remain unaffected by Peabody's patriotic zeal—least of all the impressionable young Roosevelt. In fact, Franklin was so smitten that in 1898 he made plans to run away from school to fight in the Spanish-American War. His dreams of heroism were dashed only by a last-minute case of scarlet fever.

If the flexibility, political savvy, and liberal thinking of the older Franklin Roosevelt were not learned in the halls of Groton, certainly the firm conviction of right and wrong, the patrician manner, and the sense of duty to society were largely attributable to the school's headmaster. Peabody led the church service on the morning of Roosevelt's first inauguration in 1933, and the two men maintained a close relationship. In 1942, after nine years in the White House, FDR wrote the following message to his former schoolmaster: "More than 40 years ago you said something about not losing your boyhood ideals in later life. Those were Groton ideals—taught by you—and your words are still with me."

Harvard

In 1900 Franklin became a Harvard man. Adapting to life in Cambridge, Massachusetts, presented few of the difficulties that he had faced in his first year at prep school. First of all, many former classmates matriculated with him. Second, Groton had prepared him quite well socially and academically, though classroom performance was of little concern to him. Finally, Harvard was a refreshing and exciting change from the isolated environment of Groton. The old, wealthy families of Boston-Cambridge were very much like those of the Hudson River Valley, and Franklin spent a good deal of time calling on the formidable residences of the upper crust.

Young Roosevelt was even more determined to be a social success at Harvard than he had been at Groton. Club membership was an important status symbol, and he desperately hoped to be picked. Working hard to win the respect of his classmates, he crossed the first hurdle by being tapped for a sophomore society. His confidence bolstered, Franklin set his sights on the most elite final club, Porcellian. But, as at Groton when he was passed over for senior prefect, Franklin came away disappointed. Though picked by another prominent club, Fly, he was not chosen for Porcellian. Eleanor Roosevelt later said that the whole affair left him with a bit of an inferiority complex. Franklin himself once confided to a relative that it was "the greatest disappointment" of his life.

Frustration also came on the athletic fields. Still too thin and unskilled to excel at football, he was cut from the freshman squad after two weeks of practice. He also went out for crew but did not make the team. His participation in organized sports never progressed beyond the intramural level.

Academically, Franklin's performance at Harvard was no more inspired than it had been at Groton. Content with a "gentleman's C" average, he devoted relatively little time or energy to his studies. Though he was not greatly stimulated, he did show some interest in history, government, and economics. Most apparent in his intellectual development was a growing awareness of societal commitment. While his parents and the Reverend Peabody had instilled a sense of civic responsibility, the conviction was now more mature and enlightened. In a paper written during his sophomore year, he attributed the strength of the Roosevelt family over many generations to a "very democratic spirit. . . . They have felt that being born in a good position, there was no excuse for them if they did not do their duty by the community." And it was more than lip service. Franklin regularly took his leave from the ivory tower of Harvard to teach at a boy's club in downtown Boston.

The boy's club was just one of Franklin's many extracurricular activities. A "joiner" from the start, he was a member of no less than eight clubs and organizations. He was secretary of the freshman glee club, head librarian of Fly, a cheerleader, and a staff member of the undergraduate daily, the *Crimson*. His ambition was to become the newspaper's editor-in-chief, and for once he was not disappointed. Thanks to his thorough preparation and advance work at Groton, Franklin was graduated from college in three years and devoted his fourth year to editing the *Crimson*. The paper focused primarily on routine matters of student life, but Roosevelt later called his work on it "the most useful preparation I had in college for public service."

From Hyde Park through Groton and Harvard, Franklin had little of the formal training that one might expect in a future president. He did develop high ideals, a strong sense of civic duty, and a persuasive charm. But his intellectual preparation was lacking (primarily because of his own disinterest), and he had almost no exposure to the practical side of politics—campaigning, party organization, caucuses, and the uses of power in general. He was elected to his class committee at Harvard but showed little flair even for student government.

Franklin D. Roosevelt (center, seated) was president of the Harvard Crimson, *the university's student newspaper, during his senior year (1904).*

Meanwhile, his family and personal life had undergone radical changes by the time he was ready to graduate from college. In 1900, Franklin's freshman year, his father died of a heart attack at age 72. In 1902 Sara—then only 48—took an apartment in Boston to be near her only child. Franklin was a devoted son, but he was developing opinions and feelings of which Sara did not always approve. Though he usually gave into her, two issues were becoming bones of contention. One was Franklin's budding romance with a distant cousin; the other was his growing fascination with the career of cousin Ted, the President of the United States.

Eleanor, Cousin Ted, and Politics

"I know my mind"

ANNA ELEANOR ROOSEVELT was Franklin's fifth cousin once removed. She was the daughter of Elliott Roosevelt (Teddy's younger brother) and Anna Hall Roosevelt. Elliott was one of Franklin's godparents, and Eleanor was brought on her first visit to Hyde Park at age 2. According to one account, Franklin, who was two years older than his cousin from New York City, crawled around the nursery with the girl riding on his back. The next time Eleanor visited Hyde Park she was a tall, serious 17-year-old being courted by a Harvard man who happened to have the same last name.

As secure and serene as Franklin's childhood had been, Eleanor's was unsettled and unhappy. The future First Lady—and one of America's great humanitarian reformers in her own right—was given little affection or confidence as a young girl.

Her mother, a beautiful socialite, openly expressed her disappointment at Eleanor's homeliness and lack of grace by nicknaming her "Granny." Anna was a severe, unsympathetic woman who suffered from violent headaches. She died when Eleanor was 8. Elliott, on the other hand, was warm and loving toward his "Little Nell." Eleanor adored her father but did not see him often. Elliott had a serious drinking problem, spent much of Eleanor's youth in sanitariums, and died before the girl's tenth birthday. Eleanor was reared by her strict Grandmother Hall, and she entered her teens feeling ugly, inadequate, and socially ill at ease. It was ony during her three years at Allenswood, a finishing school in England, that she gained any measure of poise and self-confidence. She made her debut in New York in 1902 but had little interest in being a belle. Having developed a strong social conscience, she devoted her time to working for the poor at a settlement house in the city. Still shy and of ordinary beauty, she was greatly flattered by the attentions of her handsome cousin.

Franklin was no stranger to the grand balls and social rituals of the East Coast elite. And while he had many young women to call on, he was taken with the sweetness and honesty he saw in Eleanor's face. As he got to know her more, he found a sensitive, concerned human being and quickly fell in love. Franklin was still at Harvard, Eleanor in New York, and their relationship was at first confined to letters and occasional weekend visits—both of which became more frequent as time went on. He invited her to Cambridge and Hyde Park, and she was happy to make the trips (always with a chaperone). Franklin, in turn, traveled to New York whenever he could get away. Their letters grew increasingly affectionate, filled with poems, confidences, and plans for when they would see each other next. In late 1903 Franklin proposed marriage, and Eleanor accepted.

Franklin's mother was surprised and disappointed. Sara knew Eleanor and liked her as a person but felt that the "children"—aged 19 and 21—were too young to be married. A widow for only three years, she was also possessive of her son's affection. She had been hoping that after college Franklin would return with her to Hyde Park. When instead he announced plans to be married, Sara did not hide her feelings. Franklin was firm with her, saying in a letter, "I know my mind." So as not to hurt his mother too deeply, however, he did agree to go with her on a Caribbean cruise to "think things over." Eleanor and Franklin spent a happy weekend in New York before the trip and exchanged letters nearly every day for the five weeks they were apart. Franklin came back more determined than ever to be married, and Sara could only give in.

The wedding was held on March 17, 1905—St. Patrick's Day—at the adjoining New York City townhouses of Eleanor's cousin Susie and great-aunt Maggie Ludlow. Reverend Peabody officiated at the ceremony, and Theodore Roosevelt came up from Washington to give away his niece. Uncle Ted had been inaugurated president only two weeks before. (He had actually been president since 1901, but his first years in office completed the term of William McKinley, who had been assassinated.) The new president arrived at the wedding amid great fanfare, and he stole the show. After the vows were exchanged, Uncle Ted drew rolls of laughter by telling Franklin that "there's nothing like keeping the name in the family." Then he strode off to the salon in a cluster of guests, leaving Eleanor and Franklin quite alone in the parlor.

After a three-month honeymoon in Europe, Eleanor and Franklin moved into a small house in mid-Manhattan, which Sara had rented and furnished for them. Franklin was now in his second year at Columbia Law School, doing little better than he had at Groton or Harvard. The New York Bar examination was offered during his third

Two years after their marriage, Eleanor and Franklin sit on the steps at Hyde Park on a summer afternoon.

year, and he managed to pass. Withdrawing from school in the spring of 1907, young Roosevelt was hired by the respected Wall Street firm of Carter, Ledyard, and Milburn even though he did not have his law degree. The first year was an unpaid clerkship, and the work was tedious. In the next two years he was assigned several important cases, including the defense of major companies in antitrust suits filed by the government. Even as a managing clerk, Franklin was growing bored and restless.

Meanwhile, for Eleanor, married life was proving a little more difficult than she had expected. She had no experience managing a household, and scrambled eggs was about all she could cook. Sara played a constant role in the young couple's life, planning and providing for them as she saw fit. Eleanor was a loving and obedient daughter-in-law, but Sara's domination of Franklin was a source of frustration. Franklin himself was hardly indulgent of his wife's shyness and insecurity. Outgoing and fun-loving, he was the life of many a party that Eleanor did not attend, left early, or watched from a quiet corner. He also spent many a weekday evening and Saturday afternoon playing poker at the University Club. (His favorite game was seven-card stud, with one-eyed face cards wild—a game requiring skill, shrewdness, and an acute sense of timing.)

Eleanor gave birth to their first child, Anna, in 1906 and their second, James, in 1907. Within the next ten years she would bear four more children—Elliott (1910), Franklin, Jr., (1914), John (1916), and one who died in infancy. It would be a difficult period for her, demanding patience with her children, submission to her mother-in-law, and devotion to her husband. Franklin, at the same time, was beginning his career as a public official.

Young Politician

Opportunity called in 1910 when Franklin was working at Carter, Ledyard, and Milburn and managing the family's Hudson River estate. A district attorney from Dutchess County, John E. Mack, visited New York on a legal matter and met with the Hyde Park native. Mack was active in the local Democratic Party, which was looking for a candidate for the state senate. Franklin appeared to be an ideal choice—young, well-bred, wealthy, and a Roosevelt. Even though Cousin Ted was a Republican, any association with the much-loved president could only win votes. Franklin had been hoping for a change in his life and was anxious to follow in the footsteps of his older cousin. He had already told several law clerks that he would pursue the same career path: Harvard, Columbia Law School, New York State legislator, assistant secretary of the Navy, governor of New York, and president of the United States. With the first two steps behind him, he jumped at a chance for the third.

It would be an uphill battle. The district had been solidly Republican for decades, and Roosevelt was a novice at the game of politics. He did not know many people in the county and was unfamiliar with their needs. For one month he campaigned furiously, growing in confidence and polish. To make contact with the voters, he employed a tactic that gave notice of his imagination and flair for the dramatic. He rented a red Maxwell touring car—the only automobile in the area—decorated it with flags, and crisscrossed the district. The automobile attracted crowds wherever he went, and the candidate was never without an audience. Voters were won over by his personal charm, gritty determination, and straightforward speeches. His strategy was ideally suited to the situation. Local politics was under the control of a small group of officials who had almost dictatorial power. Roosevelt, a new face on the scene, attacked bossism and political corruption at every turn. The young idealist apparently struck a chord with the public, winning the seat by a healthy 1,140 votes.

Having moved the family to Albany, Franklin plunged headlong into his new job. Still only 29, he had an immediate impact on the legislative session of 1911. Following through on his campaign vows to promote clean government and fight bossism, he bravely took on the powerful political organization called Tammany Hall. In those days, U.S. senators from New York were elected by the state legislature rather than by the public. Young Roosevelt quickly gained notice by leading a small group of Democratic assemblymen who opposed the Tammany candidate, "Blue-eyed Billy" Sheehan. After a bitter three-month fight, Sheehan's name was withdrawn, and a compromise candidate was agreed upon. Though it was only a partial victory for Roosevelt, the Sheehan affair was an auspicious start to his career in politics.

Roosevelt's record in Albany was one of progressive reform. He was a champion of soil conservation, aid to farmers, workmen's compensation, development of electric power, popular election of U.S. senators, women's suffrage, and a bill establishing 54 hours as the maximum workweek for boys aged 16 to 21. In substance, his goals were to help the working people of the state and return the political process to them. In style, he was brash, hardworking, personable, and shrewd. His large brownstone house was head-quarters for the anti-Sheehan campaign, and he was a master at organizing his forces, building support, and sizing up people on both sides of the fence. His supporters were devoted and ad-miring, though some members of his own party found him haughty, glib, and self-centered. He still had his "Hah-vahd" accent and a way of looking down his nose at people. Others found him heavy-handed and at times tactless. "You know," he admitted years later, "I was an awful mean cuss when I first went into politics."

Roosevelt did not plan to run for a second term in 1912, but he quickly changed his mind when he found out how badly Tammany wanted him out of office. Again he was a zealous vote-seeker, refusing to give up even when he came down with a case of typhoid in the middle of the cam-paign. Not to be denied, he turned for help to a former Albany correspondent of the *New York Herald*, Louis McHenry Howe. Eleanor and Sara took an immediate disliking to the disheveled, chain-smoking ex-reporter, but Franklin knew him to be a clever political operator. Out of a job, Howe was delighted to work for the promising young politician. He ran the campaign with as much energy and imagination as Roosevelt him-self, getting the message out in letters, posters, and newspaper advertisements. With an especially strong following among farmers and laborers, Roosevelt won reelection by a 1,701-vote margin. From then on, Louis Howe would be an indispensable adviser and close friend.

In his second term, Roosevelt resumed his progressive leadership and his crusade against bossism. In 1912 he again defied Tammany Hall, this time by supporting New Jersey Governor Woodrow Wilson for the Democratic presidential nomination. When Wilson won the party nod and then the election itself, Roosevelt was in line for a position of consequence in the new administration. Two offers were made, neither to his liking. Then, Secretary of the Navy Josephus Daniels recommended him for assistant secretary, and Franklin did not even hesitate. He had loved ships and the sea since childhood and, more important, it was the next step on Cousin Ted's road to the White House. "How would I like it?" replied Franklin to Daniels. "I'd like it bully well."

The influence of Theodore Roosevelt on Franklin's rise in politics went beyond mere ambition. The young state senator had started out with a high idealism—bred by his father and the Reverend Peabody—and his progressivism over the next two years followed the general lines drawn by Theodore. Though Franklin fought his political battles without invoking the name of his famous relative, and though Cousin Ted was a member of the opposing party, the younger Roosevelt was drawn to similar positions. Theodore had been rallying support for social and economic reforms, and Franklin recognized that the cause was both just and politically fashionable.

Franklin's emergence as a champion of social causes was also attributable in large part to Eleanor. Her abiding compassion for the poor and underprivileged no doubt influenced her husband's thinking. Eleanor saw virtue in public service and was supportive of Franklin's career in politics. Gradually she learned to manage the household, organize family vacations in Campobello, and enjoy the excitement of Albany. She participated in the endless strategy sessions at "political headquarters" downstairs, attended committee hearings, made her opinions known, and earned the respect of her husband's advisers and colleagues. Dutifully, though not comfortably, she carried out the many obligations of a state senator's wife. And while Washington would mean even more in the way of parties, receptions, open houses, and private calls, Eleanor was happy to move there as wife of the assistant secretary of the Navy.

Sara, meanwhile, had never been thrilled about her son's involvement in the "messy business" of politics. With Franklin's new appointment, however, she seemed less disapproving. Perhaps she began to realize that he simply would not settle for the idle life of a country gentleman. Or perhaps she realized that Franklin's new post was less political and more prestigious—"a *very* big job," as she described it in a letter.

Assistant Secretary

Roosevelt's new job was indeed more administrative than political. As second in command in the Navy Department, he was responsible for the day-to-day operations of a vast organization. Secretary Daniels established policy, and Roosevelt saw to it that the policy was carried out. And while he had no real experience in managing a large organization, Franklin proved an able and dedicated administrator. "I get my fingers into everything," he would say.

One of his major responsibilities was to handle the Navy's extensive and complex relations with labor unions and supply contractors. Many of the civilian workers at Navy facilities were members of a union. It was important that the Navy not give in to excessive union demands, but it was a political necessity for the Wilson administration to maintain good relations with organized labor. At the same time, Roosevelt also had to ensure that naval yards were productive, efficient, and well disciplined. It was to his credit that everyone—recruits, civilian workers, union organizers, administration officials, and congressmen—stayed happy. Naval yards were well run, with major reform measures smoothly instituted. Middlemen were cut out of the purchasing of supplies, and profiteering was squelched. Inspection tours were routine and frequent. Roosevelt ran a tight ship.

In addition to administrative experience, FDR's position as assistant secretary of the Navy gave him important contacts in Washington and the Democratic party. His political ambitions were still burning, and a growing circle of party organizers was planning great things for his future. Louis Howe, who had moved his family to Washington and was constantly at Roosevelt's side, was the most optimistic. He not only assisted Roosevelt in his duties at the Navy Department; he also kept his eye on the political horizon.

In early 1914 Roosevelt considered running for governor of New York but was dissuaded from doing so when President Wilson asked him to stay in Washington. By mid-1914, however, Roosevelt could no longer contain himself; he announced that he would seek the Democratic nomination for U.S. senator. It was a rash decision, on which not even Howe had been consulted. Despite another vigorous campaign, Roosevelt was beaten badly by the Tammany Hall candidate, James Gerard. It was a humbling experience, and the young politician learned some important lessons about party organization, the power of political machines, and his own impetuosity. It was the last time he would ever lose an election in his own right.

Back in Washington, attention was focused on the deepening crisis in Europe. Tensions had been mounting for many months, and the situation exploded in August 1914 when Germany declared war on Russia. Since coming into the Navy Department, Roosevelt had been a strong advocate of a "large and efficient Navy." Despite clashes with Secretary Daniels, who favored a less drastic military buildup, Franklin had worked hard to keep the Navy prepared. He estimated needed supplies, negotiated large contracts, gathered statistics, and made sure all facilities were in constant readiness. Now upon his return to the department, Roosevelt spoke out even more forcefully for military expansion. In his zeal, the young assistant secretary frequently overstepped his immediate superior, but Secretary Daniels was tolerant of his antics. As it turned

As assistant secretary of the Navy, Roosevelt played a key role in the U.S. military effort during World War I.

out, Roosevelt's aggressive stand was vindicated when the United States was drawn into World War I in April 1917.

With the war effort in full swing, Roosevelt played an important part in U.S. naval operations. He was given many important assignments, which he handled admirably. Recruiting and training seamen, procuring supplies, supervising naval construction, assisting with military strategy, and coordinating efforts with European allies were among his major contributions. His deepest wish, however, was to don a uniform and join in the actual fighting. Cousin Ted thought it was a "bully" idea, but Secretary Daniels felt Franklin was too valuable as an administrator. In July 1918 the secretary sent him on an inspection tour of naval facilities in Europe. During his visit, Roosevelt had a chance to meet with several Allied leaders and to see the war firsthand. He came back ready to demand military duty, but—as at Groton during the Spanish-American War—his hopes were dashed by an untimely illness, this time pneumonia. His final major task as assistant secretary was to supervise the demobilization of U.S. naval stations in war-torn Europe. He set sail in January 1919, with Eleanor accompanying him. It was during the voyage that they learned of Teddy's death.

Franklin's early years in Washington, especially during the war, would have a lasting effect on his character and political career. The administrative training and personal contacts would be invaluable. Indeed, Franklin viewed the whole experience as preparation for larger tasks ahead. He cultivated relationships with important people and tried to learn everything he could from them. His defeat in the 1914 Senate race made him a more realistic political planner, and World War I had a deeply sobering effect throughout his life.

But despite the ways in which he had matured, Franklin was still brash, cocky, and to some, still a "feather duster." Handsome and witty, he was a fixture on the Washington social circuit and was not always taken seriously. He still had a way of making light of things. According to one acquaintance, "He was likable and attractive, but not a heavy-weight. . . . He could charm anybody but lacked greatness."

Eleanor: The Transformation

For Eleanor, the early Washington years would be remembered as a period of disappointment and change. World War I marked the beginning of her transformation from a shy, private person to a committed public servant. Events in her personal life further strengthened the need to be independent and self-reliant, the need to have her own role and responsibilities.

With the outbreak of war in 1917, Eleanor joined with the other wives of Washington officials in doing volunteer work for auxiliary service organizations. It was a welcome change from the social and domestic duties that had occupied her until then. Sometimes working 18 hours a day, she was in charge of knitting at the Navy Department, worked in Red Cross canteens, helped organize the Navy Red Cross, handled mail from the troops, and introduced a food-saving program recognized by the Food Administration as ''a model for other large households.'' A hatred of war was branded in her conscience by the trip with Franklin to war-torn Europe. Seeing the death and destruction firsthand would keep her from ever again settling into a life of secluded complacency.

Eleanor's personal life also underwent a radical change. As the wife of an important official, her volume of mail increased so drastically that in the winter of 1913–14 she was forced to hire a social secretary, Lucy Page Mercer, 22. Franklin was frequently away from home, and he rarely accompanied Eleanor and the ''chicks'' to Campobello or Hyde Park. When he could be at home, Louis

Howe always seemed to be with him. The early romance of Eleanor and Franklin had never developed into a close, sharing relationship, and now they seemed to be moving even farther apart. Sara didn't help. She competed for the affection of the children and still doted on Franklin. Eleanor's status was symbolized by her tiny bedroom in the refurbished Hyde Park mansion, squeezed in between the large, commodious rooms of her mother-in-law and husband.

In September 1918 Eleanor's world came completely apart. Franklin had just returned from his tour of Europe and was bedridden with pneumonia. While unpacking his luggage, Eleanor discovered a packet of letters—love letters—from Lucy Mercer. Franklin had always referred to the pretty secretary as ''the lovely Lucy'' and to herself as ''Granny,'' but she had never thought anything of it. Now Eleanor realized what was going on, and nothing could have wounded her more deeply. She had borne Franklin's six children, and her entire world revolved around him.

Eleanor confronted her husband with the letters, and Sara was called in for a family conference. Franklin admitted that he was in love with Lucy and wanted to marry her. Eleanor said he could have a divorce if he did not think the children would suffer too greatly. If he wanted to stay, however, he would have to promise to stop seeing Miss Mercer. Sara was furious at her son and told him she "would not give him another dollar" if he didn't end things with the secretary at once. Beyond the children and beyond money, Franklin was also concerned about the consequences a divorce might have on his career in politics. Whichever weighed most heavily on his mind, he agreed never to see Lucy Mercer again.

The marriage, however, was irreparably damaged. Eleanor later said, "I can forgive, but I cannot forget." Now more than ever, she realized that she would have to live her own life and stand up for herself. She joined charitable organizations, established new programs for the needy, and took up a host of humanitarian causes. Through the ordeals and triumphs of coming years, Eleanor and Franklin developed great mutual admiration, even devotion, but never the deep affection of their youth.

4

Polio and a Governorship

"We must go forward or flounder"

FRANKLIN'S RISE TO prominence had been swift and impressive. Still only 38, he had made a name for himself in Albany and Washington, gaining the recognition of powerful politicians and behind-the-scenes organizers. If sometimes he was perceived as a bit soft around the edges, his ten years in public life had given him a hard core of confidence, conviction, and political savvy. His battles with Tammany Hall and disagreements with higher-ups in Washington had taught him that diffidence and compromise were sometimes the most prudent course. He had learned that a politician must cultivate a public image, projecting his own best qualities and putting the best face on everything that might be associated with him. His greatest asset was his ability to adapt to new situations and remain on good terms with people of competing needs. He worked hard to project charm, vitality, and strength of character. By 1920 the unique combination of lion and fox—courage and cunning, strength and savvy—was beginning to emerge. In the next ten years there would be new lessons for the fox and a test of courage for the lion.

After his return from the European sweep-up operation, Franklin's interest in politics was rekindled by the upcoming elections of 1920. In mid-1919 he began speaking out on national policy, Democratic party politics, and a variety of social issues. With the ever-present Louis Howe, he drafted recommendations for the party platform that were typically progressive. Roosevelt was still very much a Wilson man, but the president had suffered a paralyzing stroke and had come up against strong Senate opposition to his most cherished goal: establishing a League of Nations. The Democrats would be choosing a new candidate, and the prospects of that candidate would be dim at best.

At the party convention in San Francisco in June 1920 Roosevelt gave a seconding speech on behalf of New York Governor Al Smith, who ultimately withdrew from the nomination contest. Then Roosevelt threw his support to William G. McAdoo, Wilson's treasury secretary. On the forty-fourth ballot, Governor James M. Cox of

Ohio finally won the party's nomination. To Franklin's surprise, and Louis Howe's dismay, Roosevelt, himself, was the choice for vice-president. Back at Hyde Park, he gave his first speech as a candidate for national office. ''We can never go back,'' he said. ''The 'good old days' are gone past forever; we have no regrets. . . . We must go forward or flounder.''

The Cox-Roosevelt ticket was doomed from the start. Wilson had called for the 1920 elections to be a ''solemn referendum'' on the League of Nations, and public sentiment was against him. Cox and Roosevelt favored the League and made it the central issue of their campaign, but the people were fed up with Wilson, the Democrats, and the idea of the League. There was nothing Roosevelt loved more than a good fight, and he gave this one his all. It was an extensive and exhausting campaign that touched every part of the country. Franklin, accompanied by Eleanor and a team of aides, followed the campaign trail by train, automobile, and even airplane. On ''whistle-stop'' train tours across the country, he gave more than a thousand speeches from caboose platforms. With increasing eloquence, he spoke not only for the League of Nations but also for conservation of natural resources, farm benefits, labor reform, and other progressive policies.

But his efforts were to no avail. In November the Republican ticket of Warren G. Harding and Calvin Coolidge won by a landslide.

Franklin was disappointed by the severity of the defeat, but he had gained much from the experience. The loss was more a repudiation of Democratic traditions and Cox's candidacy than of the vice-presidential running mate. After World War I, the nation was ready for a return to Republican ''normalcy''—which Harding had called for—and Roosevelt could hardly be faulted for that. Indeed, his efforts in the campaign established him as a national political figure to be contended with in the future. Additional benefits were the associations he established with several hardworking aides. Among them were Stephen Early and Marguerite (Missy) LeHand, both of whom would hold key positions in the Roosevelt White House. Moreover, in the long hours and close confines of the whistle-stop tours, Eleanor and Louis Howe had grown to be friends. They confided in each other, consulted one another, and developed a strong mutual trust. Finally, Roosevelt learned another lesson in the subtle art of politics. Supporting the League of Nations, like fighting Tammany Hall, was a self-defeating strategy. He felt strongly about both, but being a lion wasn't enough. He had to be shrewd enough to distinguish popular issues from political suicide.

When the enemy is strong, don't fight him head on. Befuddle him. Outfox him.

With conservative Republicans controlling Washington and the nation wanting a "return to normalcy," Roosevelt had no choice but to return to private life and wait for another chance. It was a boom period for American business and a good opportunity to make some money. Eleanor and Franklin had always been thrifty, but now they had five children and two households to maintain, one in New York City and the other at Campobello. And while both Eleanor and Franklin had substantial inheritances, now was a chance for additional security. Franklin joined a small law partnership, which eventually became Emmet, Marvin, and Roosevelt. He was named a vice-president of a large surety bonding firm, called the Fidelity and Deposit Company of Maryland. Willing to take risks and try out new things, he also invested in a variety of business ventures—oil, forestry, electricity, resort hotels, and even lobsters. In addition to his business activities, he was president of the Navy Club, chairman of the Boy Scouts of New York, an overseer of Harvard, and an organizer of the Woodrow Wilson Foundation. It was a busy time for him, but he still had high hopes for his political future.

Then the hope faded.

Ordeal

The Roosevelt cottage at Campobello was a thirty-room summer house with no heating system, wicker furniture, and a wide front porch for reading and idle conversation. Like Hyde Park, it was a place Franklin had loved since early childhood. It was a place to relax, sail, and be with his family. In the summer of 1921 Franklin was tired and anxious to return to the isolated island retreat. In August, Van-Lear Black, the president of Fidelity and Deposit, offered to take him there on his yacht, the *Sabalo*. Franklin quickly accepted. In the Bay of Fundy the *Sabalo* ran into foul weather, and Franklin was forced to stand at the wheel for several hours. The next morning they went cod fishing, and Franklin fell overboard. He later said he "never felt anything so cold as that water." On his first day at the cottage, Roosevelt took the children sailing and from the middle of the bay noticed a forest fire on a nearby island. He landed the boat and rallied the children to beat out the flames with tree boughs. Then they went for a swim in a lake, ran 2 miles back toward the house, and took an ice-cold dip in the bay. When they got home, Franklin sat in his wet bathing suit reading the mail.

The next morning, his legs felt limp, and he developed a fever. When the limpness turned to

After polio left his legs paralyzed, Roosevelt found that swimming was the best exercise. From 1924 to the end of his life, he made frequent visits to Warm Springs, Georgia, to bathe in its natural mineral water.

pain and his temperature rose, a doctor was called in. He said it was a simple cold. When Franklin lost all feeling in his legs and lower back, an expert diagnostician was sent for. He said it was a blood clot and prescribed massage. Eleanor and Louis Howe, who had been invited along for the vacation, rubbed his feet and back for days. It didn't help. Only after two weeks did another specialist make the correct diagnosis: poliomyelitis, or infantile paralysis.

In mid-September Franklin was sent by private railroad car to New York City and Presbyterian Hospital. He spent six weeks there, but his condition did not improve. The specialist in charge, Dr. George Draper, feared that he would never be able to sit up, let alone walk. Franklin was at first depressed, but for the sake of others he managed to put on a facade of cheerfulness. It was the politician in him.

He also believed that with hard work he would someday be able to walk again. With patience, the help of family and friends, and endless exercising, he did get back on his feet—albeit with the help of leg braces. And though eventually he could walk with crutches, he never gave up searching for a complete cure. Swimming proved to be the best exercise, and in 1924 he began bathing at the health resort of a friend in western Georgia called Warm Springs. The mineral water helped enormously, and Franklin spent many weeks there. In 1926 he bought Warm Springs for some $200,000—about two-thirds of his personal fortune—and developed it into a leading polio-therapy center.

How polio altered Franklin's character and the extent to which it affected his career are difficult to determine. Certainly it was the greatest test of strength, patience, and determination he would ever face. Any challenge he ever confronted would always be kept in perspective. When later asked whether events at the White House ever worried him, he replied: "If you had spent two years in bed trying to wiggle your big toe, after that anything else would seem easy!" Max Lerner, a noted magazine editor, said the ordeal developed in him "a sense of mastery over himself and others." According to Eleanor, FDR's famous pronouncement that "the only thing we have to fear is fear itself" was based on deep personal experience.

For a politician, being handicapped presented special problems. Howe insisted that he never be carried in public, and the press was ordered never to photograph him from the waist down. For campaigns and other public appearances, Roosevelt eventually had a custom-made Ford Phaeton with special hand controls. At the same time, being crippled was also a political asset. It won respect, sympathy, and votes from the public. If nothing else, it was an easy excuse for not attending boring political functions.

Down But Not Out

In the early stages of his recuperation, the long hours Franklin spent with his stamp collection and model ships gave him valuable time to think and assess the future. And while he still had no keen ideological insights, he did see that the period of his convalescence was not a good time for Democrats, anyway.

From the beginning of his illness, Sara urged her son to retire to Hyde Park and live there in secluded comfort. Eleanor and Franklin both disagreed. Eleanor felt that he needed to return to normal activity as soon as possible, and Franklin was determined to rehabilitate himself. As for Louis Howe, his high hopes for the political future never waned. "By gad," he declared, "legs or no legs, Franklin will be President." Eleanor, Howe, and Missy LeHand took over his affairs and did everything they could to help him in his fight.

As his energy returned, Franklin took up several activities in law and business. He ended his association with Emmet, Marvin, and Roosevelt, striking a new partnership with a lawyer named Basil O'Connor. He speculated in several new commercial enterprises and was made president of the American Construction Council. That association had been set up to bring order into the building industry so as to avoid government regulation. As its president, Franklin gained important insights into government-business relations.

More importantly, Roosevelt also kept his political contacts. Eleanor made stand-in appearances at various organizational gatherings and party functions. Franklin and Howe wrote hundreds of letters to Democrats all around the country, offering advice, giving inspiration, and congratulating them on election victories. At the 1924 Democratic convention, Roosevelt dragged himself to the podium at New York's Madison Square Garden and made a dramatic seconding speech for his political ally Governor Al Smith. He called Smith the ''happy warrior,'' but the nickname seemed more appropriate for himself. The *Herald Tribune* called Roosevelt ''the real hero'' of the convention. Smith lost the nomination for the second time, and in November, the Republican candidate, Calvin Coolidge, won the presidency. The Democrats were clearly in disarray, and Roosevelt went to work trying to reorganize the party. And though his efforts were largely unsuccessful, he was greatly uplifted by the work.

In New York Al Smith was still governor. He urged Roosevelt to run for the U.S. Senate in 1926, but Franklin did not want to give up his rehabilitation or his commitment to Warm Springs. He did continue to work for the party, and in 1928 he gave yet another seconding speech for Smith at the Democratic National Convention. Foreseeing the political importance of radio, he wrote his speech with a home audience specifically in mind. It was a skill that would prove valuable in years to come.

This time Smith won the nomination, but his chances against Herbert Hoover in the election did not look good. The Roaring Twenties were in full swing, and the Republicans were riding the crest of prosperity. Smith knew it was vital to win his home state of New York, and he had an idea to bolster his chances there. If the much-admired Roosevelt were running for governor, his own candidacy would be given a boost. Howe was against it, and Franklin did not feel ready. But party pressure continued to mount, and FDR finally gave in.

Governor Roosevelt

The 1928 New York gubernatorial campaign was a personal triumph for Franklin Roosevelt. The Republican opposition raised questions about his health and depicted him as the puppet of his predecessor, Al Smith. Roosevelt answered any doubts about his personal well-being with a vigorous campaign. Showing all the vitality of earlier years, he set out in mid-October on a train tour of the southern part of the state. Then, wanting closer contact with the people, he switched to an automobile. Wearing the same battered hat in which he had campaigned for the vice-presidency in 1920, he delivered up to seven speeches a day from the back of his car and in crowded auditoriums. His bout with polio had made him a stronger man and a more magnetic candidate. It was a new beginning.

On the morning after the election Roosevelt and Smith were in New York City to find out the results. They were mixed. Smith had been beaten badly, even losing New York by 100,000 votes. Unaffected by the Republican landslide, however, Roosevelt had defeated Albert Ottinger by 25,564 votes.

On January 1, 1929, FDR took the oath of office at the state assembly building in Albany. It was the same room in which Cousin Ted had been sworn in as governor thirty years before.

Roosevelt began his two-year term with an inaugural address in which he called for an "Era of Good Feeling." That would not be easy. There was a Republican majority in the legislature, and even the most moderately progressive legislation would be contested. Roosevelt also had a falling out with Al Smith, who wanted a major role in

On January 1, 1929, FDR was sworn in as governor of New York State. The preceding election was disappointing for Democrats across the country, but FDR won his election by 25,000 votes.

the decision-making process even though he was no longer in office. The new governor followed the general lines of his predecessor's administration, but he wanted to make his own decisions. Sam Rosenman and James Farley were newcomers who quickly won important responsibilities. Eleanor was active as an "ombudsman" for the state, fielding complaints from the public and trying to find solutions.

During his tenure as governor, Roosevelt fought for a broad range of reforms in the areas of agriculture, conservation, and labor. His efforts in social policy were a taste of the things to come during his presidency. His most cherished legislative proposals provided for old-age pensions, prison reform, tax relief for farmers, a 48-hour workweek for women and children, reforestation of abandoned farmland, and modernization of government. Many of his initiatives were stalemated or watered down by the Republican legislature, but he did have important successes. Certainly his political skills were being sharpened. In his battles with the legislature, he employed a tactic that in coming years would change the American political process for all time: going directly to the public via the media. "It seems to me," said Governor Roosevelt in 1929, "that radio is gradually bringing to the ears of our people matters of interest concerning their country which they refuse to consider in the daily press with their eyes.'' The public apparently liked what it heard. In 1930 Roosevelt was reelected by some 725,000 votes, the largest margin in state history.

Of deep concern to Roosevelt during his second term, however, was the collapse of the economy. The stock market crash of October 1929 had started an economic disaster in New York and all around the country. No governor took it more seriously or acted on it more decisively than FDR. He was the first governor to set up an effective state relief administration. The program was run by a former social worker named Harry Hopkins, who would become a vital member of the Roosevelt team. With his industrial commissioner, Frances Perkins, Roosevelt devised an unemployment insurance system and created jobs on state conservation projects. At a time when drastic action was called for, Roosevelt mobilized the state government with firmness and clever tactics. He was determined to have his way, and most often he did. The Depression was a national catastrophe, and the actions of a single governor could hardly solve all the problems, even in his home state. But by focusing his energies on the plight of the poor, Roosevelt won the deep affection of the people of New York.

All in all, Governor Roosevelt exhibited many of the policies and practices that he would later employ as president. In style, he was as determined to get what he wanted, as open to the advice of close aides and outside experts, as calculating, as tough, as vibrant, as friendly, and sometimes as hard to figure out. His efforts in such areas as labor reform, agricultural assistance, and land conservation would be elaborated and expanded in the White House years. His economic programs in New York were the forerunners of the New Deal.

Indeed, Roosevelt had been thinking ever more seriously about the presidency. His spectacular election victory in 1930 and the failure of the Republican administration made him a promising candidate. James Farley may have jumped the gun when, after the 1930 landslide, he said: "I do not see how Mr. Roosevelt can escape becoming the next presidential nominee of his party." Franklin did not object. Once again Louis Howe wrote to Democrats all across the country, and party organizers began rounding up support.

On January 23, 1932, one week before his fiftieth birthday, FDR formally announced his candidacy. Sam Rosenman convinced him that he had better start some policy planning, and Roosevelt began putting together a team of advisers that would become famous as his "Brain Trust." Said candidate Roosevelt in a radio address that April: "These unhappy times call for the building of plans . . . that put their faith once more in the forgotten man at the bottom of the economic pyramid."

Faith in the Forgotten Man would be the theme of his campaign and the hallmark of his presidency.

The Presidency—First Term

"I pledge you, I pledge myself, to a
new deal for the American people"

IN JULY 1932, twenty-two years after barnstorming
Dutchess County in a red Maxwell touring car,
Franklin Roosevelt flew to Chicago to accept the
Democratic nomination for president of the
United States. His appearance shattered political
tradition. No other Democratic nominee had ever
gone to the party convention, let alone by airplane. Days of political infighting had taken a lot
out of the delegates, but the surprise entrance of
their champion set off a wild din.

In the months before the convention, FDR had
stood out as the most dynamic and imaginative
candidate. With Farley and Howe managing his
campaign, Roosevelt won primary elections in
several midwestern and far western states. In
speech after speech, he attacked the business
community, called for drastic changes in the eco-

nomic system, and promised bold experimentation. His calls to action roused support throughout the country and gave him a decisive lead over the other candidates. Still, his opponents attacked him for being wishy-washy and vague. They pointed to his noncommittal stand in the Walker-Tammany scandal and his reversal on the League of Nations issue. (Roosevelt was now opposing the League.) Moreover, Roosevelt was intentionally vague in his campaign promises, and the opposition called him to task. Despite his early lead, then, Roosevelt was never a shoo-in for the nomination. The winning candidate would need two-thirds of the delegates behind him, and Roosevelt lost important spring primaries in Massachusetts and California. At the convention, he came out far ahead on the first three ballots but did not win the required two-thirds majority. In a crucial move, Farley offered the vice-presidency to John Nance Garner of Texas if he would turn over his delegates to Roosevelt. Garner agreed, and FDR won the nomination on the fourth ballot.

Dressed in a blue suit with a red rose in his lapel, the crippled candidate moved slowly to the rostrum and greeted the cheering delegates. His decision to come to Chicago, he said, was ''unprecedented and unusual, but these are unprecedented and unusual times. Let it be from now on the task of our party to break foolish traditions." In a lengthy speech, he attacked the Republican leadership and called for a brave new recovery program. Emphasizing the need for work and security, he outlined some of his remedies for the economic ailments of the nation. "I pledge you," he concluded, "I pledge myself, to a new deal for the American people." A great roar rose from the floor of the convention, and the band struck up "Happy Days Are Here Again."

FDR was the clear favorite in the presidential race. The disaster of the Republican administration would have made any Democrat a promising candidate, particularly since the Republicans were sticking with President Hoover as their nominee. Hoover had battled the Depression without success for three years, and he appeared defeated and glum. One observer remarked: "If you put a rose in Hoover's hand it would wilt." Roosevelt, by contrast, radiated warmth, vitality, and easygoing confidence. Democratic senators even suggested that their candidate stay at home and not jeopardize his lead with a full-fledged campaign. Roosevelt would hear nothing of that. "My Dutch is up," he told Farley.

The candidate set out on a grueling cross-country tour, taking with him an entourage of aides, advisers, speech writers, party officials, and experts in every area of national concern—especially the economy. Devoting each major speech to a specific issue, he outlined several aspects of his New Deal, including relief, public works, farm price stabilization, conservation, and unemployment insurance. For the most part, however, he remained intentionally fuzzy. As the decided front-runner, he thought it more prudent not to go into great detail on such controversial topics as labor legislation, industrial recovery programs, and foreign policy. Hoover called him a "chameleon on plaid," and many others were alienated by his lack of specific ideas. But Roosevelt knew the game of politics. He cleverly outfoxed his opponent, attacking him from all sides and staying clear of any traps. In November Roosevelt won 42 states to Hoover's 6; 472 electoral votes to Hoover's 59; and 22,815,539 popular votes to Hoover's 15,750,000. The Democrats also took firm control of the Senate and House.

The four months between the election and the inauguration were the worst of the Great Depression. After three years of hard times, the American people faced another long winter without enough food, clothing, or shelter. Bewilderment had turned to fear, anger, and finally hopelessness. As the ranks of the unemployed swelled to

13 million, faith in the system dwindled to nothing. It looked like the death of the capitalist system. And things got worse. More banks closed. More companies shut down. President Hoover was at wit's end, and Congress did not know what to do.

Roosevelt, meanwhile, was calm and optimistic. He spent much of his time at the Little White House in Warm Springs, choosing a cabinet and planning policy. He refused several invitations by Hoover to join in emergency action. He lobbied the support of various factions around the country, but he still gave few specifics about his programs. Tensions were heightened by an assassination attempt in mid-February 1933. On a crowded street in Miami, Roosevelt sat in his car with several aides and supporters. A short, dark man named Giuseppe Zangara, an unemployed bricklayer, began shouting from the crowd: "I hate the rich and powerful. . . . Too many people are starving to death!" In a frenzy, Zangara opened fire at Roosevelt's car. The president-elect was not hit, but the mayor of Chicago, Anton Cermak, was fatally wounded. The unflappable Roosevelt showed no loss of composure.

As the inauguration approached, America was still wondering what kind of leader it was getting. Roosevelt had been elected out of despair and

After being sworn in as president on March 4, 1933, FDR tells The American people that "the only thing we have to fear is fear itself."

seemed to have few definite plans, but his confidence and bold promises gave hope.

In a Washington hotel room FDR put the final touches on his inaugural address. On a nearby shelf lay a book of essays by Henry David Thoreau, in which Roosevelt read the words: "Nothing is so much to be feared as fear." Seized by the simple expression of optimism, he penned his famous statement: "The only thing we have to fear is fear itself."

The Hundred Days

The morning after his inauguration, the new president rose early, ate a quick breakfast, and had himself wheeled into the Oval Office. The room was empty except for the presidential desk and chair. The desktop was clear, the drawers empty. There was not so much as a pencil or pad of paper, and Roosevelt sat alone and helpless. He looked for a buzzer, but there was none. Finally he yelled for a secretary and work got under way.

The first order of business was to save the nation's banking system. In his speech the day before Roosevelt had asked for "broad Executive power to wage a war against the emergency." Now it was time to act. In the afternoon he called a meeting of the cabinet to set his plans in motion. Within four hours the president issued two proclamations: one called Congress into an emergency session beginning four days later; the other declared a nationwide "bank holiday." All banks would be closed and all transactions suspended until formal recovery measures were passed by Congress.

For the next four days, the administration worked without rest on legislation to revive the banks. Meanwhile, the holiday itself was easing tension. The mere fact that action was being taken bolstered the nation's spirits. By the time Congress returned, Roosevelt had a bill ready. It was not a radical reformation of the whole banking system, as some people expected, but it did extend government assistance to private bankers, put all banks under federal control, and set up an inspection committee that could authorize the reopening of "sound" banks. The House passed the bill before it even got copies, the Senate approved it a few hours later, and the president signed it into law that evening. By the middle of the month, three-fourths of all banks in the Federal Reserve System were reopened.

Roosevelt had originally intended to send Congress home after it had passed the banking bill, but the legislators approved it so readily that the president decided to push for more. The next day he proposed a $500 million cut in the federal budget to reduce inflation. This, too, was passed. Then he exerted pressure by going directly to the people. On Sunday, March 12, one week after taking office, he held his first Fireside Chat. With 60 million Americans listening, he explained his banking policy in simple terms and asked for the public's cooperation. "Confidence and courage," he told them, "are the essentials of success in carrying out our plan." The speech was a hit. With homely metaphors and a conversational delivery, Roosevelt made every listener feel as if he or she were being talked to personally. The ability to go over the head of Congress was a valuable political asset, and Roosevelt knew it. During his twelve years in the White House, he gave a total of twenty-eight Fireside Chats.

With Congress in special session for 104 days, FDR pushed through bill after bill. During this period he sponsored no less than fifteen major legislative proposals and thirteen other laws. As humorist Will Rogers said: "The whole country is with him, just so he does something. If he burned down the Capitol, we would cheer and say, "Well, we at least got a fire started anyhow.'" The Hundred Days, as it became known, marked the beginning of the New Deal.

Roosevelt had some definite ideas about what had caused the Depression and what permanent changes needed to be made in the U.S. economic system, but the goal of the early New Deal was first to provide emergency relief. Long-term reforms could not be instituted until the nation was at least partially back on its feet. The result of his first years in office was a hasty, hodgepodge series of recovery measures. From the beginning, there was no grand design for the revival of the economy. Roosevelt's style of leadership was to surround himself with advisers who had diverse and competing points of view, listen to their opinions, and try everything. The first years of his presidency were a buzzing confusion of programs, proposals, plans, and policies. During the Hundred Days alone, Congress established countless new agencies, represented by a confusing jumble of initials: CCC, FCA, FERA, AAA, TVA, HOLC, FDIC, and NRA.

Relief and Recovery

Roosevelt's early relief initiatives were directed toward as many different constituencies as possible. The rapid succession of new programs represented his desire to be president of all the people, to serve all segments of society. To be a successful leader and politician, he would need the backing of as many groups as he could win over. This was also reflected in the cabinet he chose. There were Democrats and Republicans, liberals and conservatives, northerners and southerners, and, for the first time, a woman— Secretary of Labor Frances Perkins. Another carry-over from the administration in Albany was Postmaster General James Farley. Cordell Hull was secretary of state; Harold Ickes was secretary of the interior; William Woodin secretary of the treasury; Henry Wallace secretary of agriculture; Homer Cummings attorney general; and Daniel Roper secretary of commerce. With the help of Vice-President John Nance Garner, the Brain Trust—including Rexford Tugwell, Raymond Moley, and Adolph Berle, Jr.,—as well as Eleanor, Louis Howe, Sam Rosenman, Missy LeHand, Stephen Early, and scores of others, Roosevelt sought to pull the country from the depths of despair.

One of FDR's favorite early New Deal projects was the Civilian Conservation Corps (CCC). At its peak, the CCC employed 500,000 young workers to reforest public land, build flood-control structures, and improve the nation's parks. Another important agency was the Federal Emergency Relief Administration (FERA), which provided federal funds to state-run employment programs. The Reconstruction Finance Corporation (RFC) offered loans to large and small businesses. The

Home Owners Loan Corporation (HOLC) gave help to mortgage-holders in distress. The Public Works Administration (PWA) undertook such large-scale projects as highways and public buildings, specifically for the purpose of creating jobs. And the Civil Works Administration (CWA) hired skilled workers and craftsmen.

The operations of the CWA and PWA typified the early New Deal in spirit and substance. The Civil Works Administration was the idea of Harry Hopkins, who believed that the government could afford to hire as many as 4 million workers to do all kinds of part-time jobs, whether they were needed or not. Within one month after its formation, the CWA had hired 2.6 million people. After just two months, Hopkins had reached his goal of 4 million. No job was too small or trivial for the CWA. One group of researchers was hired by the agency to study the history of the safety pin. ''Boondoggle'' became the new word for a seemingly useless or wasteful activity that the government paid for.

The PWA, meanwhile, was based on a different approach. The Public Works Administration was the idea of Harold Ickes, who believed that every federal dollar should be spent on *worthwhile* jobs. Anything else, he felt, was demeaning to the worker. In six years, 1933–39, the

PWA spent $6 billion on such projects as the Grand Coulee Dam in the state of Washington, the Triborough Bridge in New York, the sewage system in Chicago, and thousands of schools throughout the country.

The rivalry betwen Ickes and Hopkins was exactly the kind of atmosphere Roosevelt loved. He encouraged competition between novel ideas. He was a great experimenter, and the best evidence of this was the existence of different programs with the same ultimate purpose.

While the CWA, PWA, and other agencies accomplished the important goal of putting people to work, the heart of the early New Deal recovery effort was the Agricultural Adjustment Agency (AAA) and the National Recovery Administration (NRA). Both were created in the Hundred Days of 1933. Roosevelt believed that imbalances in agricultural and industrial production were a major cause of the Depression. Many commodities were being overproduced, resulting in low prices and meager incomes. The AAA was designed to limit agricultual output and restore farm prosperity. The NRA was created to curb industrial production and promote cooperation between government and business.

In sending the AAA legislation to Congress, Roosevelt called it a "new and untrod path." The

AAA actually paid farmers to reduce their acreage and limit their crops. Production quotas were established for seven basic commodities. If farmers stopped producing once the quotas were reached, they would be given special subsidies, or monetary grants. Limits on production meant higher farm prices. These increases, along with the government subsidies, restored the purchasing power of farmers. The program was popular among farmers, but it had only limited success. Small, temporary improvements did occur in the agricultural sector, but the overall picture was not really healthy until the 1940s.

The NRA bill, according to the president, was "the most important and far-reaching legislation ever enacted by the American Congress." The National Recovery Administration, under the leadership of General Hugh (Ironpants) Johnson, was to administer codes of "fair competition" in individual industries. The agency encouraged management and labor to negotiate production and pricing policies in exchange for collective bargaining, guaranteed minimum wage, and maximum work hours. Under the aegis of General Johnson, hundreds of NRA codes were written in a few short months. The program was purely voluntary and could be carried out only through public pressure. Johnson designed the famous

Blue Eagle as the NRA symbol, and it appeared in store windows everywhere. Johnson urged every American housewife to have the Blue Eagle "on everything that she permits to come into her home." In September 1933, some 250,000 marchers paraded down Fifth Avenue in New York City to celebrate the NRA. More than 22 million workers and 2 million employers were eventually covered by NRA codes.

Of all the New Deal initiatives, the NRA probably had the greatest and most immediate effect on the American people. It did much to coordinate overall industrial production, prices, wages, and working conditions. At the same time, however, the NRA also typified the weaknesses and inadequacies of the entire New Deal. Another grand experiment, the NRA was overly ambitious and ill planned. The system grew increasingly complicated and unmanageable. The more than 500 codes could not be effectively enforced. There was a spurt of industrial recovery in the summer of 1933, but the boom quickly died. The business community blamed Roosevelt. In May 1935 the U.S. Supreme Court declared the National Industrial Recovery Act (NIRA) unconstitutional. This set the stage for the major political battle of FDR's presidency, to culminate during his second term.

The relief and recovery measures of the early

New Deal underscored the major strengths and weaknesses of Roosevelt's leadership. Individually and collectively, these programs showed that the president was a flexible and dedicated man of action. He was an aggressive statesman and charismatic politician. He pushed Congress and instilled confidence in the people. At the same time, his programs seemed random, ill considered, and sometimes inconsistent—indeed, *too* flexible. Roosevelt was also proving to be a cautious politician, sometimes ignoring needed programs so as not to alienate certain groups. For example, he recognized the need for sweeping civil-rights legislation, but fearing a loss of support from southern Democrats, he initiated none. In terms of the economy itself, he held back from large-scale federal spending or any major assumption of control by the government.

All in all, the early New Deal was moderate and conservative in character. The emphasis was on practical measures rather than on radical ideological change. The results were mixed. The Depression was by no means over, and rumblings of discontent were heard from certain groups. On the other hand, the economy was showing definite signs of life, and the majority of Americans believed deeply in what their president was doing.

Reform

The midterm elections of 1934 were a show of support for President Roosevelt, with the Democrats gaining ten seats in the Senate and House. Nevertheless, there was growing opposition from both ends of the political spectrum. On the right, the business community attacked him for excessive government spending and giving in to unions, and the wealthy accused him of being a traitor to his class. On the left socialists blamed him for not being enough of a reformer.

The president seemed more concerned about the opposition from the left. The business community and the upper-class had been longtime enemies, and he had won many a vote with his tough stand against them. But now there were new voices calling for radical changes in the American system, social as well as economic. Among the most outspoken and influential of these men were Senator Huey Long of Louisiana, Father Charles Coughlin of Michigan, and Dr. Francis E. Townsend of California. Each of them advocated social programs that went far beyond anything Roosevelt had instituted. Each of them was vehement in his attacks on the president. Together they started a movement that FDR could not ignore.

In late 1934 and early 1935 Roosevelt changed his tack. Whereas the early New Deal had sought quick relief and short-term recovery, now his programs would focus on long-term rehabilitation. The emphasis shifted from conservative stopgap remedies to a deliberate program of social reform. The zigzag was a shrewd political maneuver that Roosevelt used time and again to outsmart his opponents. But his motives were not entirely political. The Depression was far from over, and a new strategy was worth trying. The early New Deal had been characterized by efforts to reduce production and raise prices. Now Roosevelt would try to increase consumption and raise purchasing power. His new approach would attack the same problem from a different angle.

At the heart of the New Deal reform effort were several important new agencies: the Tennessee Valley Authority (TVA), Securities and Exchange Commission (SEC), Federal Deposit Insurance Corporation (FDIC), Social Security Board (SSB), National Labor Relations Board (NLRB), and Works Projects Administration (WPA). All except the WPA are still active.

The Tennessee Valley Authority (TVA) and Federal Deposit Insurance Corporation (FDIC) had actually been formed in 1933, but both were fundamentally reform initiatives. The TVA was created to develop an entire region through its water resources. This large-scale program provided flood control and cheap hydroelectric power by building multipurpose dams. It manufactured fertilizer, promoted soil conservation, and helped in regional planning. The FDIC, enacted during the busy Hundred Days, was designed to prevent a run on the banks. The agency provided federal insurance for all deposits under $5,000.

The Securities and Exchange Commission, created in 1934, was the first step by the U.S. government to control the stock market. Some experts believed that the Depression had been caused in part by fraudulent stock dealings during the 1920s. The SEC now required all new stock issues to be registered with the government. The agency would closely monitor the day-to-day affairs of Wall Street.

The Wagner Act, passed in 1935, was the most important labor legislation enacted to date. It guaranteed labor unions the right to bargain collectively on equal terms with management, and it created the National Labor Relations Board (NLRB) to rule on any labor dispute. Largely because of this legislation, the labor movement expanded significantly during the 1930s and 1940s.

Also passed in 1935 was the Social Security Act, which began a whole new trend in American government—welfare. The 1935 law provided for federal old-age pensions, as well as federal cooperation with individual states on relief for the needy, disabled, blind, and unemployed.

In further assistance to the unemployed, the government created a new jobs program—the Works Projects Administration (WPA). This agency soon became the nation's largest single employer, hiring an average of 2.1 million workers a year and spending $11 billion between 1935 and 1943. Under the guidance of Harry Hopkins, the WPA undertook such massive projects as New York's La Guardia Airport and the St. Louis waterfront. The real purpose of the agency, however, was to hire skilled and semi-skilled workers for similar jobs in their own trades. These included everything from digging ditches to writing plays

Beyond the new relief agencies, beyond regulatory commissions, and beyond public-works projects, President Roosevelt pushed for other important changes during his first term. Prohibition was repealed, the dollar was taken off the gold standard, and a novel tax measure was instituted whereby big corporations and wealthy individuals were subject to greater levies. All in all, the New Deal would have lasting, far-reaching effects on American government and the American way of life. Washington would have tighter control over private enterprise and greater responsibility for the economic and social well-being of the people.

In the meantime, the remedies prescribed by Dr. New Deal, as Roosevelt called himself, were proving moderately successful in combating the Depression. By the time he was up for reelection in November 1936, FDR could point to real improvements in the economy. The gross national product had increased by about 40 percent since 1932, and unemployment had been reduced by 2 million. Although there were still some 10 million unemployed, and although complete recovery was yet far off, the economy had grown by a steady rate of about 15 percent annually since late 1934. Despite criticisms from the left that Roosevelt had not done enough—and from the right that he had gone too far—the nation was clearly in better condition than it had been on the day he was sworn in. Disaster had been averted.

Politically, Roosevelt had been a masterful strategist. He had staved off the opposition from both sides by zigzagging a middle course. His New Deal programs had forged a strong alliance of farmers, laborers, and the underprivileged. Business and financial leaders, leftists, and newspaper editors fulminated against "That Man in the White House." They complained that he was inconsistent, dishonest, and a madcap experimenter. Most Americans, however, believed the president when he began his Fireside Chats with the words "My Friends." Since he had proclaimed a "day of national consecration" four years earlier, Franklin Roosevelt had won many new supporters with his personal charm, political maneuvering, and real accomplishments.

The result was a stunning victory over Alfred M. Landon, the governor of Kansas, in the 1936 election. In fact, it was the greatest landslide in more than a century. Roosevelt was returned to office by winning 523 of 531 electoral votes. His 27,752,309 popular votes far outdistanced Landon's 16,682,524. FDR carried every state except Maine and Vermont, and the Democratic party increased its already large majorities in both houses of Congress.

At the moment of his great triumph, Roosevelt could hardly foresee the troubles he would encounter during his next four years in the White House.

The Second Term

*"To maintain a democracy of effort
requires a vast amount of patience . . .
a vast amount of humility"*

FRANKLIN ROOSEVELT LOVED being president. He relished the power. He thrived on the challenge. His aides and assistants marveled at the enthusiasm with which he went about his daily routine. Over an early breakfast, he would scan a half-dozen newspapers and hear the impressions of his "Missus," who traveled around the country acting as his "eyes and legs." He spent hours on the phone every day, coaxing congressmen, soliciting advice, pressuring opponents, and negotiating political deals to strengthen his position. He was constantly calling in staff members or advisers, and he held press conferences twice a week. He usually had one drink before dinner and worked in his office for a few hours before retiring.

When he wasn't working, Franklin presided over life at the White House like the gentleman squire of a Hudson River Valley estate. He loved sailing the Potomac on the presidential yacht, the *Nourmahal*. He relaxed in an old tweed jacket that his father had given him and which he later handed down to one of his sons. The Roosevelts enjoyed hosting dinner parties, but without the elaborate trappings and stiff formality previously seen in the White House. Franklin loved to eat wild game and usually carved it himself. When the king and queen of England visited Hyde Park in 1938, they were served hot dogs. Eleanor's specialty was still scrambled eggs, which she cooked every Sunday night she was home. The rooms of the presidential mansion were decorated simply, and neither the president nor the first lady went in for fancy clothes. (Franklin allowed himself only two new pairs of shoes each year.) Anna, Jimmy, and Elliott were grown up and visited whenever they could. The Roosevelt grandchildren had nurseries on the third floor and a sandbox and jungle gym on the South Lawn. Franklin, Jr., and Johnny were teenagers, coming and going as they pleased, much to the chagrin of the White House guards. For the Roosevelts, 1600 Pennsylvania Avenue was a home as much as an official residence. It exuded all the warmth and cheerfulness that so many loved in FDR himself.

The usually reliable "Roosevelt weather" did not come through for the second inauguration in January 1937. It is unlikely that Franklin saw this as an omen. With the success of his first term and his landslide reelection, he was more sure of himself than ever. As the rain poured down, Roosevelt took full credit for the economic improvements over the previous four years. Through his actions, he boasted, "stagnation and despair" had been ended. "In these last four years," he went on, "we have made the exercise of all power more democratic. . . . Our progress out of the Depression is obvious." Then, in perhaps the most memorable words of his speech, he conceded that the crisis was far from over: "I see one-third of a nation ill-housed, ill-clad, ill-nourished." In vintage Roosevelt rhetoric, he rededicated himself to the battle for universal prosperity: "The test of our progress is not whether we add more to the abundance of those who have much; it is whether we provide enough for those who have too little." And in a stirring call for unity, he pledged his own good faith and asked the same of the people: "To maintain a democracy of effort requires a vast amount of patience in dealing with differing methods, a vast amount of humility."

Like so many of his other speeches, the second inaugural address was an opportunity for Roosevelt to teach and defend the moral certainty of America's "long-cherished ideals." So firm was his belief in democracy that every oration sounded like a civics lesson and a sermon rolled into one. In the tradition of his cousin Ted, FDR viewed the presidency as a "bully pulpit," an excellent platform from which to preach high ideals. As early as 1932 he had declared that "the presidency is preeminently a place of moral leadership."

As he began his second term, however, Franklin Roosevelt seemed to lose sight of some of those ideals. The problem was overconfidence. He scorned his enemies and made excessive demands of his supporters. During the campaign he had baited the business community and the Republican party, saying: "I *welcome* their hatred!" In his inaugural address he promised patience and humility, but nothing was more lacking throughout his second term. His astute sense of timing, willingness to compromise, and personal persuasiveness seemed lost. Out of stubbornness or for revenge, he acted against his own best interests time after time. Uncharacteristically, he made serious mistakes in political strategy. And the more he was resisted, the more power he sought. As much as he still loved being president, he was a frustrated man during his second four years in office.

The Court-Packing Scheme

The lines of the first major battle had actually been drawn in May 1935 when the Supreme Court declared the National Industrial Recovery Act (NIRA) unconstitutional. In a case called *Schechter Poultry Corp.* v. *United States,* the justices ruled that the NIRA gave the president too much power and that it violated previous judicial holdings regarding "interstate commerce." Roosevelt was furious. He called the ruling a "horse-and-buggy definition of interstate commerce," implying that the judges were too old-fashioned and conservative. He thought they were interfering in his New Deal program and standing in the way of economic recovery. Roosevelt's outrage was compounded in January 1936 when, in *United States* v. *Butler,* the Court also declared parts of the Agricultural Adjustments Act (AAA) unconstitutional.

It is uncertain when Roosevelt began planning his revenge, but he waited until the second term to launch his attack. Two weeks after the swearing in, Chief Justice Charles Evans Hughes and the other members of the Court were invited to the White House for their annual dinner. The mood was light and friendly.

Two days after that, on February 5, Roosevelt announced to Congress his plan to "reform" the

Supreme Court. The judiciary was overburdened with work, he maintained, and something had to be done. For every justice who refused to retire within six months of his seventieth birthday, the president would be allowed to appoint a new member, up to a maximum of six. It just so happened that six justices were already beyond 70 years old. That would allow the president to expand the body from nine to fifteen members, thereby alleviating the problem of overwork. More importantly, Roosevelt believed that his plan was necessary to override the Court's conservative majority, which had threatened the New Deal programs so desperately needed by the American people. In a Fireside Chat on March 9, the president pointed out that Congress has the power to change the number of Supreme Court justices and indeed had done so in the past. "I hope that you have re-read the Constitution of the United States in these past few weeks," he told the people. "Like the Bible, it ought to be read again and again." Once more Roosevelt was sounding like a preacher.

The Court proposal was fiercely resisted. Few saw it as an honest, good-faith effort to promote the democratic process. Most saw it as an attempt by a frustrated president to "pack" the Court with his own men and have his way on every issue. The public and members of his own party were aghast at the transparency of his revenge. The opposition screamed "Dictator!"

The debate was at a fever pitch for several months, but the proposal was doomed from the start. "Too clever. Too damned clever," wrote a newspaper that had supported the New Deal. Chief Justice Hughes wrote a letter to the Senate, showing clearly that the Court was in no way overburdened. Democratic leaders in Congress were upset about not being consulted before the plan was announced. The Republicans were determined to strike their first heavy blow against the president. In April the Supreme Court further weakened Roosevelt's cause by *upholding* two other New Deal initiatives, the National Labor Relations Act and the Social Security Act. By midsummer, the "Court reform" scheme had been overwhelmingly rejected.

All that could be said for Roosevelt's plan was that the Supreme Court did seem to adopt a more lenient approach to liberal legislation. It began interpreting the Constitution more broadly, opening the door for more government regulation. Other than that, little good came of the plan. In fact, it was, probably the biggest political blunder of Roosevelt's career. It began a breakdown of his support and lent credence to the rabid denunciations of his critics. The great irony of it was that FDR eventually made seven appointments to the Court through the traditional procedure.

Low Tide

The true "happy warrior," Roosevelt tried to remain cheerful in the face of adversity. As attacks by the Republicans, business community, and far left grew more severe, the president tried to keep his confidence and sense of humor.

"You undergraduates who see me for the first time," he told a college audience in North Carolina, "have read in your newspapers and heard on the air that I am, at the very least, an ogre—a consorter with Communists, a destroyer of the rich, a breaker of our ancient traditions. . . . You have heard for six years that I was about to plunge the Nation into war; that you and your little brothers would be sent to the bloody fields of battle in Europe; that I was driving the Nation into bankruptcy; and that I breakfasted every morning on a dish of 'grilled millionaire.'

"Actually, I am an exceedingly mild-mannered person—a practitioner of peace, both domestic and foreign, a believer in the capitalistic system, and for my breakfast a devotee of scrambled eggs."

But, as the tide of Roosevelt's popularity began to recede, he was having a hard time hiding his anger and frustration. He lost his temper with cabinet members, poked fun at Vice-President Garner, and criticized the press. General Hugh Johnson, who had been fired from the NRA in 1934 and had become an anti-New Deal newspaper columnist, was called to the White House to have it out with the president. According to Roosevelt, ''Ironpants'' Johnson was reduced to tears.

What stung Roosevelt most deeply was the loss of support from congressmen and senators of his own party. Throughout his first term, more than a few Democrats had felt pressure to support the president's entire economic package even if they disagreed with certain parts. But the Supreme Court plan was an issue on which they would not be bullied. They were disenchanted by Roosevelt's stubbornness, and important bills had taken a back seat to the debate over Court reform. The president had postponed legislation on work hours and wages, agricultural development, low-cost housing, and other social-economic measures. As political allegiances in Congress began to waver, the president exerted more pressure, and the disenchantment grew even deeper. Although several new agencies were authorized and

reform measures passed during Roosevelt's second term—including the Farm Security Administration, U.S. Housing Authority, and Fair Labor
Standards Act—most proposals were killed some-
where along the congressional path.

The Court fight and a restive Congress were
not FDR's only problems. Labor unions were also
beginning to cause headaches. As a result of New
Deal legislation and Roosevelt's long-standing
support of the labor movement, workers began
organizing as never before. Union problems began creeping up in the automobile, steel, and
other mass-production industries. The number of
strikes had risen from about 1,700 in 1933 to more
than 4,700 in 1937. Many of them ended in vio-
lence. At the same time, militant workers had
resorted to a new tactic: the "sit-down" strike.
Roosevelt opposed sit-down strikes, but by the
summer of 1937 he was nevertheless taking much
of the blame for the labor unrest. The business
community was more anti-Roosevelt than ever
before. Conservatives throughout the country felt
increasingly alienated. As union membership
skyrocketed, more and more of the middle class
was turning Republican. To make matters worse,
left-wing liberals were shocked when, during a
steel strike, Roosevelt told labor leader John L.
Lewis and the steel companies: "A plague on *both*
your houses."

Adding to FDR's woes was a sharp economic downturn in the fall of 1937. The recovery had been steady and substantial since 1932, largely because of federal relief and loan programs. Early in 1937, however, Roosevelt began thinking that the government was spending too much money and running up too large a deficit. In an effort to balance the budget, he drastically reduced federal spending. As a result, the economy took a sharp turn for the worse. Unemployment rose, production and sales declined dramatically. Economic indicators fell almost to the levels of 1932, and the downturn was immediately labeled the "Roosevelt recession." Taken aback, the president quickly increased government expenditures. By June 1938 a measure of stability had been restored, but the whole episode had been another severe blow to FDR's prestige.

By January 1939 President Roosevelt's popularity and political clout had reached a low-water mark. His domestic policies were stalemated in Congress, and the legislators opposed him more strongly than ever. Congressional committees were investigating several New Deal agencies for improprieties. Presidential appointments faced stiff opposition. There was even public criticism of the First Family. Mrs. Roosevelt was condemned for extensive traveling and outspoken support of liberal causes. Sons James and Elliott were criticized for taking advantage of the family name in business. And a series of divorces by the Roosevelt children were grist for the gossip columnists. Amid all these troubles, FDR also had to begin facing up to the crises brewing in Europe and the Far East.

The Foreign Front

On January 30, 1933, only five weeks before Franklin Roosevelt was first sworn in as president of the United States, Adolf Hitler was appointed chancellor of Germany. As leader of the National Socialist Workers' (Nazi) party, he had won a national election with the support of conservative industrial, agricultural, and military groups. When Hitler came to power, Germany was also suffering from the Great Depression. The new chancellor was given almost unlimited authority, and he put a vast number of people to work building superhighways and other impressive projects. At the same time, he was building a one-party totalitarian state. In powerful and convincing speeches, he proclaimed to the German people that they were naturally superior to all other races. As the economy got stronger, the citizens backed their chancellor more fervently. Hitler gradually tightened his grip on the government, and when President Paul von Hindenburg died in 1934, he assumed that office as well. It was then that Hitler began looking beyond Germay's own borders. With the rise of Nazism in Germany, Italian Fascist dictator Benito Mussolini also seemed to become bolder. In 1935 he launched an attack against Ethiopia, and the following year he made a heavy commitment in the Spanish Civil War. And in the Far East, the militaristic Japanese regime turned its back on international cooperation after taking over Manchuria in 1931.

The United States, meanwhile, was decidedly isolationist during the New Deal era. That is, it sought to separate itself from international affairs. The president, the Congress, and the public were more concerned about solving the economic problems at home. During his first term, FDR's foreign policy was intended primarily to facilitate and strengthen U.S. trade, to promote international cooperation, and to avoid excessive involvement on the world scene. In 1933 he resisted the advice of outgoing President Hoover to deal with the Depression as an international problem. That July he delivered his famous ''Bombshell Message,'' saying that the United States would not participate in the London Economic Conference on international currency stabilization. In November Roosevelt formally recognized the Soviet

Union in the hope that this would increase trade. Reciprocal trade agreements with several other countries broke down tariff barriers. A mutual Good Neighbor Policy with Latin American nations promoted international cooperation, but it hardly thrust the United States to the forefront of world affairs. In August 1935 Congress passed the first in a series of Neutrality acts, establishing conditions and restrictions on any U.S. participation in foreign conflicts.

President Roosevelt did not entirely share the isolationist sentiments that lay behind the neutrality legislation. Though he was most concerned with getting his New Deal programs through Congress, he was becoming more and more wary of the threat from overseas. Cautiously, so as not to alienate Congress or the voters, he took steps to ensure military preparedness, exert pressure in Europe and Asia, and alert the public to the gravity of the situation. In 1935 he formally discouraged the sale of raw materials to Italy during the Ethiopian War. In 1936 he budgeted the relatively large sum of $1.2 billion for military purposes. And in October 1937, after Japan had begun a new push southward into China, he delivered a speech in which he called for a "quarantine," or enforced isolation, of any aggressor nation. As so many times during his second term, FDR was roundly criticized. With isolationist sentiment still strong, the speech was considered by many as a step toward war.

By 1938 developments in Europe forced Roosevelt to focus more and more of his attention on foreign policy. In March Hitler "annexed" Austria. Then in September the Fuhrer browbeat France and Great Britain into letting him take over the Sudetenland—a region in Czechoslovakia—in exchange for a false promise of peace. Roosevelt had long recognized the threat of Nazi aggression, but now he had neither the political power nor the popular backing to take the actions he thought necessary. In early 1939 he petitioned Congress for a revision of the most recent neutrality legislation, which had imposed an arms embargo on all nations at war, whether the attacker or the attacked. He was turned down.

In September 1939 Hitler overran Poland and war was declared in Europe. Roosevelt called Congress into special session to revise the Neutrality Act, and this time he was successful. The embargo on arms sales to warring nations was repealed. Weapons and ammunition could be sold on a "cash and carry" basis. The president's hands were still tied, but finally there was some room for maneuvering.

1940: Elections and Entanglement

For three years the most pondered question in Washington was whether Franklin Roosevelt would run for a third term as president. Either he had made a decision he thought wiser not to divulge or he was genuinely unsure of what to do. In any case, even his closest aides could not be certain until the summer of 1940, just before the Democratic convention. Factors working against him were the breakdown of his wide-based political support and the long-standing tradition that a president should not serve more than two terms. A large anti-third term movement opposed his candidacy on the grounds that another four years would be "dictatorial." Moreover, after the Court reform controversy, the Roosevelt recession, the 1938 congressional election debacle, and other political embarrassments, FDR appeared to be an ineffectual "lame duck" president.

Working in favor of Roosevelt's candidacy were his still formidable talents as a political tactician and the ever-worsening international situation. By staying out of the early campaign, the president was actually strengthening his position. There were so many other aspirants for the Democratic nomination that party members could reach no firm consensus on the most appropriate candidate to back. And even though the president's overall popularity remained relatively low, each ominous development in Europe lifted his standing in the polls. By mid-June, the Germans had taken over Poland, Finland, Norway, Denmark, Luxembourg, Belgium, the Netherlands, and France; the American people were beginning to recognize the gravity of the situation across the Atlantic. All the while, Roosevelt remained characteristically serene and confident. When he finally let it be known that he would seek reelection, the Democratic party was solidly behind him. His nomination was overwhelming.

The year 1940 was in many ways the most important and most telling of Franklin Roosevelt's twelve-plus years in the White House. Had it gone differently, he likely would have been remembered as a rather ordinary president, with a successful first term and a wholly unsuccessful second term. Instead, it marked the turning point and a new beginning for one of the great presidents in U.S. history. More than any other year of his presidency, 1940 bore witness to FDR's leadership ability, political flexibility, and willingness to engage in deceitful practices to achieve his goals for the nation.

The dangerous and peculiar circumstances of 1940 required that Roosevelt perform a three-way juggling act. On the one hand, Great Britain now stood alone against the Nazi menace, and Roosevelt knew that England's defeat would be an imminent danger to the United States itself. He would therefore have to come to Britain's aid and strengthen U.S. defense forces. On the other hand, public sentiment at home did not allow him to alter his basic anti-war posture. Congress and the people favored "all aid short of war," and the radical isolationist movement was still strong. Finally, Roosevelt had to contend with Republican candidate Wendell Willkie, who was winning isolationist support with his own firm pledges to keep the nation out of a conflict.

The great success of FDR in 1940 was to come to Britain's aid and increase U.S. defense without scaring the public and without jeopardizing his chances in the election. In mid-May he asked for and received from Congress $1.2 billion in additional military appropriations, as well as permission to build 50,000 combat planes a year. Later that month he set up the seven-man National Defense Advisory Commission (NDAC). In June he asked Congress for a "two-ocean Navy." In July he got another $4.8 billion in military appropriations. And in his most important and controversial move, he announced in September that he had sent fifty overaged destroyers to Great Britain in exchange for a lease on eight British military bases in the Western Hemisphere. The president announced the deal as "a good horse trade," but he came under attack for having made it without the consent of Congress. Republicans and the press called the act deceitful and, again, dictatorial.

To underscore his desire for peace, Roosevelt announced that he would never send American boys to fight in a foreign war. To quell the Republicans, he appointed two new members to his cabinet, both from the opposition party: Henry L. Stimson as secretary of war and Frank Knox as secretary of the Navy. While the latter move appeared to be a dramatic political conciliation, it was in fact a clever ploy. Coming on the eve of the GOP convention, the appointments took some of the thunder out of the Republicans' speeches. It was Roosevelt the Fox at his slyest.

Wendell Willkie proved to be a formidable candidate. Like Roosevelt, he was personally charismatic and won votes with his charm and air of confidence. The Republican challenger criticized President Roosevelt for dishonest tactics and indecisive management. The New Deal was not seriously challenged, and in foreign affairs the two opponents voiced the same position: keep America out of war. In Willkie's favor was the anti-third term tradition, but this was not enough. Those who feared war most strongly sided with Willkie, but the growing Nazi threat led most others to vote for FDR and his new vice-presidential running mate, Henry A. Wallace of Iowa. The result was 449 to 82 in the electoral college, and 27,243,466 to 22,304,755 in the popular vote. Franklin Delano Roosevelt became the first American president ever to be elected to a third term.

Even though FDR won reelection handily, his anxiety over the outcome was reflected in the somewhat unsavory tactics to which he resorted. Key Republican candidates for Congress were put under secret surveillance, and Willkie himself was considered for a smear campaign. The president had a recording device hidden in his desk lamp in the Oval Office, and conversations were taped for a period of several months. In one, Roosevelt told an aide to plant the rumor that Willkie was having an illicit affair with a woman in New York City. "Spread it as a word-of-mouth thing," the president said. Although there is nothing to indicate that the mission was ever carried out, the conversation revealed the darker side of FDR's political tactics.

In the months after the election, President Roosevelt sought to strengthen the nation's military forces, harden its foreign policy, and unify public opinion on the war issue. The latter task would be the most difficult. Four years earlier, at the Democratic convention of 1936, FDR predicted that "this generation of Americans will have a rendezvous with destiny." Now he could see that his words had been prophetic. The problem was to convince the rest of America before it was too late.

The Third Term

"With confidence in our armed forces, with the
unbounding determination of our people, we will
gain the inevitable triumph—so help us God"

WITH HIS ELECTION in 1940, FDR in effect became a
war president. No U.S. soldiers were actually in
combat, but the commander in chief acted as if
the enemy were already mapping its strategy—
which he knew it was. In December, on the
strength of his election mandate and the heavy
military appropriations from Congress, Roosevelt
pledged to make the United States "the great
arsenal of democracy." Plans for extending the
New Deal were set aside, and factories were put
to work manufacturing weapons. When asked
about economic or social policy, the president replied: "It's there on the shelf. It will have to
wait."

One of the great ironies of the Roosevelt presidency was that World War II did more to end the

Depression than the New Deal itself. Military conscription, enacted in September 1940, solved the unemployment problem as the WPA, PWA, and CWA never had. Arms production and wartime mobilization rebuilt collapsing industries and revived dying cities. The federal government grew larger and more powerful than even the most ardent New Dealer would have ever dreamed.

Equally ironic was the extent to which World War II benefited Roosevelt politically. There would always be opposition, but in the national emergency Congress was solidly behind him and the Supreme Court allowed a vast expansion of presidential authority. Indeed, the war made Roosevelt more than a political power broker, more than a military commander. He became the standard-bearer for all Americans. He was the leader and partner of every man, woman, and child in the defense of freedom and decency. He was, as he always wished to be, ''president of all the people.''

Most ironic of all, however, was the fact that the opportunity for greatness was not of Roosevelt's own making. The Congress and public were against full U.S. intervention in the war until the attack on Pearl Harbor. In November 1941, one month before the Japanese raid, a public-opinion poll showed that only 20 percent of the American people favored a declaration of war against the Axis. When Franklin Roosevelt was sworn in for his third term, Pearl Harbor was still almost a year away. Britain was fighting for its life, but the American president could not directly intervene on its behalf. Despite all his efforts, the opportunity for greatness did not really come until December 7, 1941.

Darkening Clouds

The difference between Franklin Roosevelt in 1940 and Franklin Roosevelt in 1941 was that the latter had received a strong vote of confidence from the electorate. He would still keep the United States on the sidelines of the war, and he would still need popular and congressional support for any decisive action in aid of the European democracies. But Roosevelt the Lion was not entirely in chains. With the Republican challenge soundly defeated, he could act more freely.

His first major initiative of the third term was the Lend-Lease plan, submitted to Congress in January 1941. The bill gave the president power to supply military equipment to any nation whose defense he considered vital to that of the United States. He could send any defense articles he deemed necessary, on any terms he deemed appropriate—sale, transfer, exchange, lease, or lending. Lend-Lease was intended primarily as a means of providing material to Great Britain after its cash and credit were used up. The proposal set off another heated debate in Congress and brought new accusations of dictatorship and manipulation. Manipulation it was. Lend-Lease was presented as an alternative to war, but FDR hoped that congressional backing would give him an even stronger mandate for further intervention. By agreeing to a few minor alterations in his original proposal, Roosevelt won out. Congress enacted Lend-Lease, and the president signed it into law on March 11.

Emboldened by his victory, Roosevelt set the nation on a course of action for which he did not always seek congressional approval. Like the destroyer deal with Great Britain in 1940, several of these measures were intended to step up American involvement without debate on Capitol Hill. For example, to protect arms shipments from German submarines, the U.S. Navy escorted Allied supply ships part way across the Atlantic. As it turned out, however, these "patrol" vessels were in fact convoys of destroyers. En route across the ocean, the destroyers helped pinpoint German submarines, which Allied warships then

attacked. By late fall the United States was em-
broiled in an undeclared war on the high seas,
with Congress and the public unaware. When in
September a German submarine fired on the
U.S. destroyer *Greer*, Roosevelt went before the
American people feigning surprise. He ordered
American vessels to sink any hostile German
warship.

In Europe, meanwhile, Nazi forces swept
through Yugoslavia and Greece in mid-April.
Hitler broke his nonaggression treaty with the
Soviet Union on June 22, when he launched a
massive attack against that country. The Russian
army, caught unprepared, was pushed steadily
back. Great Britain had withstood the first Nazi
air onslaught in 1940, but its position was still
precarious.

The United States was the last hope for a free
Europe, and Roosevelt knew it. Lend-Lease was
extended to the Soviet Union, and various other
steps were taken to help Great Britain. In addition
to sending destroyers into the Atlantic, Roosevelt
assisted the British in the defense of Iceland and
Greenland by establishing an American military
presence on both strategically located islands.

In August 1941 President Roosevelt and British
Prime Minister Winston Churchill held a secret
meeting off the coast of Newfoundland on the

U.S. destroyer *Augusta*. The two leaders had had extensive communications for many months, but they had never actually met. "At last," said Roosevelt, welcoming his British counterpart, "we've gotten together." For three days they discussed war aims and strategies, and although there were no firm decisions or commitments, the meeting began a friendship that would be the cornerstone of the Western alliance throughout World War II. On the last day the two leaders signed a press release proclaiming the Atlantic Charter. This was a statement of principle on the creation of a better world upon the defeat of Nazi Germany. The compelling, eight-point program for peace called for national self-determination; freedom of the seas; equal access to world trade and resources; freedom, safety, and greater economic prosperity for all peoples; and postwar disarmament.

Isolationists in the United States bitterly attacked the president for his "secretive and dictatorial" actions. Senators Robert Taft, Gerald Nye, and Burton Wheeler, as well as such outspoken private citizens as Charles Lindbergh, insisted that Roosevelt had disregarded the democratic process and illegally committed the nation to war. Their complaints were muted once and for all on December 7, 1941.

Pearl Harbor

Japan, bound by treaty with Germany and Italy, sought to take advantage of the European crisis by expanding its empire in the Far East and expelling the Western powers. Acting to contain Japanese expansion in China and Indochina, President Roosevelt in 1940 terminated all commercial agreements and embargoed all vital trade goods. These sanctions proved effective. Japan was forced to make a decision: either halt its expansion or go to war with the United States. Negotiations were held, but Roosevelt and Secretary of State Cordell Hull refused to make any concessions.

At 7:55 A.M., Sunday, December 7, 1941, Japan launched a surprise attack on the U.S. Naval Base at Pearl Harbor, Hawaii. The Japanese sought to destroy the U.S. Pacific Fleet, and its primary targets were eight battleships docked at the base. Hundreds of Japanese planes dive-bombed the harbor, and within two hours they had accomplished their mission. The *Oklahoma* and *West Virginia* were capsized, the *Arizona* was in flames, and the five other battleships were seriously damaged. A total of 18 ships and 188 planes were destroyed or rendered inoperable. American casualties were staggering: 2,403 killed or missing and 1,178 wounded. Simultaneously, the Japanese had launched attacks on the Philippines, Guam, Wake Island, Midway, Hong Kong, and Malaya.

President Roosevelt reacted calmly to the news. He was angry but not totally surprised. Although Japanese negotiators were still in Washington seeking a lifting of the trade embargo, the U.S. government had recognized that war was likely. Several historians have even suggested that FDR knew the attack was coming and allowed it to happen as an excuse to bring the United States into the war. Only months before, Roosevelt had told Secretary of the Treasury Henry Morgenthau that he was "waiting to be provoked" by some incident. Other events in the fall of 1941 suggest that the president may have known in advance about the attack. If he did, he seriously misjudged the outcome. Even if he did not, as commander in chief he had to share part of the blame for the lack of preparedness.

The day after Pearl Harbor, President Roosevelt appealed to Congress for a declaration of war against Japan. He spoke firmly and with a sense of urgency. "Yesterday, December 7, 1941—a date which will live in infamy—the United States of America was suddenly and deliberately attacked by naval and air forces of the Empire of Japan."

One day after the Japanese attack on Pearl Harbor—''a day that will live in infamy''—FDR signs the Declaration of War against Japan. Congressional leaders look on.

Denouncing the strike as "treachery," he called for an all-out commitment to absolute victory. "With confidence in our armed forces, with the unbounding determination of our people, we will gain the inevitable triumph—so help us God. I ask that Congress declare that since the unprovoked and dastardly attack by Japan on Sunday, December 7, 1941, a state of war has existed between the United States and the Japanese Empire."

Within 33 minutes of the president's message, war was declared. Three days later, on December 11, Germany and Italy declared war on the United States. Congress responded in kind.

"Dr. Win-The-War"

Franklin Delano Roosevelt was at his greatest in facing up to a crisis. His vigor, determination, and confidence shone through more brightly and more inspiringly than in the ordinary course of affairs. That his leadership qualities were better suited to a national emergency had already been made clear in his first and second terms. Now faced with the gravest foreign threat ever mounted against the United States, FDR responded in character. Ever the moralist, he inspired the American people to join together in defense of democracy, to do whatever was necessary to defeat the forces of tyranny. In his annual Message to Congress on January 6, 1942, he roused the nation with his closing statement: "No compromise can end the conflict. There has never been, there can never be, successful compromise between good and evil. Only total victory can reward the champions of tolerance and decency and freedom and faith."

Declaring at a news conference that "Dr. Win-the-War" had replaced "Dr. New Deal," FDR undertook the planning and management of the massive war effort. The first orders of business were to step up war production and begin mapping strategy. Following his usual administrative style, Roosevelt listened to a wide range of opinions before making his final decisions. But because immediate action was needed, the president relied more heavily on just a few close advisers. James F. Byrnes was put in charge of war production. Secretary of State Cordell Hull advised on matters of diplomacy. And Harry Hopkins was indispensable in coordinating all phases of the war effort. On matters of military strategy, Roosevelt relied heavily on Secretary of War Henry L. Stimson, General George C. Marshall, the Army chief of staff, and Admiral Ernest J. King, the chief of naval operations.

Thanks to Roosevelt's efforts over the previous two years, U.S. war production at the time of Pearl Harbor already equaled that of Germany and Japan combined. However, the Navy had suffered a critical blow at Pearl Harbor, and matériel would be needed by all Allied nations in both Europe and the Pacific. Upon the declaration of war, therefore, the United States set out on a war production effort unprecedented in history. It gradually amassed the largest and most powerful naval force known to man. In 1942 alone, 600 merchant vessels were launched. Eventually there would be 26 aircraft carriers, 114 escort carriers, 48 cruisers, 203 submarines, and hundreds of other vessels. Also in 1942, U.S. factories turned out 60,000 military aircraft, double the number produced the preceding year.

As the war machine began to build up American strength, Roosevelt also had to decide where to use it. From the outset, Prime Minister Churchill was consulted on overall military planning. The British leader was enormously relieved to have the United States in the war—despite the circumstances—and he arrived in Washington two weeks after Pearl Harbor for consultations on

strategy. He hoped the United States would con-
centrate its effort in Europe, and he was pleas-
antly surprised by Roosevelt's concurrence. The
American president had already determined that
Hitler was the main enemy and victory in Europe
the primary objective. Despite the fearful defeats
sustained in the Pacific, the Navy would try to
contain the Japanese as long as possible, hoping
for a gradual reversal. After a more massive effort
in Europe had defeated Hitler and Mussolini, full
attention could be paid to Japan.

Unlike Winston Churchill, Roosevelt did not
interfere in the day-to-day decisions of military
command. He had the final word on overall strategy and was kept abreast of all developments, but
the actual running of the war was left to the
leaders of the armed services. In General Marshall and Admiral King he had two exceptional
commanders, who in turn appointed their most
trusted officers to lead U.S. forces into battle.
General Dwight David Eisenhower was named to
head the Army in the European theater. Replacing
the admiral who had been caught by surprise at
Pearl Harbor, Admiral Chester Nimitz was chosen
to lead Navy operations in the Pacific.

President Roosevelt, meanwhile, concentrated
on negotiations with America's allies. From the
outset, he took the lead in establishing and for-

tifying a mutually cooperative alliance among all nations fighting the Axis. Dominating the alliance was a close partnership between Roosevelt and Churchill. The two leaders met ten times during the war: on the *Augusta* in August 1941; at Washington in December 1941, June 1942, and May 1943; at Casablanca in January 1943; at Québec in August 1943 and September 1944; at Cairo in November 1943; at Teheran in November-December 1943; and at Yalta in February 1945. In coordinating their war efforts and planning the postwar world, the president and prime minister had some thorny differences of opinion. For example, Churchill sought to postpone any large-scale U.S. invasion of France, and Roosevelt believed that British colonialism should be curtailed after the war. Despite their disagreements, the two statesmen developed a deep mutual respect and warm personal friendship. During Churchill's stays at the White House, they would spend long hours in serious discussion, often in the company of Harry Hopkins, and then relax before dinner. Roosevelt would mix the cocktails, and Churchill would wheel his friend to the table.

Following Britain's lead, the United States invaded North Africa in November 1942, Sicily in July 1943, and the Italian mainland in September 1943. In a coordination of effort that the Axis powers never effected, American and British forces finally overcame German General Erwin Rommel in North Africa. German and Italian troops put up a fierce resistance in Italy, but the Allies finally overcame with a combined force of Americans, British, Canadians, Free French, Brazilians, New Zealanders, Poles, South Africans, and others. The Fascist government of Benito Mussolini capitulated on July 25, 1943, and over the next year the Allies drove steadily up the Italian peninsula. In Northeastern Europe, the Soviet army stood alone in trying to stave off the Nazi offensive. In some of the bloodiest fighting of the war, the Russians were pushed back to Stalingrad in the summer and fall of 1942. Then in November they began a counteroffensive that proved to be a turning point in the war. By 1943 the German Sixth Army was destroyed. In the Pacific, meanwhile, the turning point had come on June 4, 1942, in the Battle of Midway. The bulk of the Japanese fleet had set sail to confront the U.S. Navy in a major surprise offensive. But the U.S. command had broken the Japanese code and was prepared for the onslaught. The Japanese fleet was decimated, and the Allies began their westward counteroffensive. It was the reversal they had been hoping for.

The Home Front

On his sixtieth birthday—January 30, 1942—a public-opinion poll showed that a whopping 84 percent, of the American people approved of President Roosevelt's leadership. The nation was united in the war effort and had thrown its full support behind FDR. On certain domestic issues, however, the president was running into some vexing opposition. Congress discontinued the WPA and other New Deal agencies, and it resisted plans for health insurance and aid to education. Especially irksome to the president was resistance to his Emergency Price Control bill. Designed to fight inflation, this war measure gave the federal government power to set prices on all goods except farm products. Finally winning congressional support, the president signed the bill into law—also on his sixtieth birthday.

Racial tension was also mounting during the early 1940s. Roosevelt had yet to take any major steps to end racial inequality, and the black community was growing restive. A march on Washington was threatened in 1941, and Roosevelt responded by creating the Fair Employment Practices Committee (FEPC). The committee was intended to prevent discrimination in defense-related industries. Although it was the most important civil-rights initiative of the entire Roosevelt presidency, the FEPC did not have much power or much success. Blacks, other ethnic groups, and the poor were still the backbone of Roosevelt's political support, but the third term did see a measure of disenchantment.

Finally, in an interesting turnaround, the president was being criticized for his *support* of the business community. With the approach and outbreak of war, Roosevelt sought a new climate of cooperation with private industry, as well as a mutuality of effort among private corporations. Companies were offered huge government contracts and generous tax breaks. The power of big business was a frequently heard complaint.

End Game

Meeting at Casablanca in January 1943, President Roosevelt and Prime Minister Churchill agreed on the goal of unconditional surrender by the Axis powers. The purpose of that decision was to avoid the confusion and disagreements that had occurred after World War I among the victor nations. When the policy was announced, however, the Axis was far from defeated. Moreover, there were some basic disagreements among the Allies, the most important of which had to do with the Soviet Union.

With the Americans and British winning in North Africa and Italy, and with Russia turning the tide at Stalingrad, the Allied leaders began focusing their attention on strategies to end the war in Europe and on plans for international order in the postwar era. Like a chess match in which three players are on one side, the United States, Great Britain, and the Soviet Union had to agree on an "end game" that satisfied each of them. Not all of them were happy with the way the game had been played so far. Soviet leader Joseph Stalin was angry because the U.S. delay in mounting a "second front" against Hitler had left the Soviet Union carrying the brunt of the fighting. Churchill persuaded Roosevelt to postpone such an invasion for two reasons: first, he thought the drive through North Africa and Italy was a better early strategy; and second, he distrusted the Soviet Communist dictator. Roosevelt went along with Churchill because he did not want to alienate him and because he was not sure an invasion was feasible yet. He was also wary of Stalin, who had divulged few of his plans despite heavy U.S. aid under Lend-Lease.

The three leaders finally met in the Iranian capital of Teheran from November 28 to December 1, 1943. Roosevelt used all his personal charm to win Stalin's friendship and faith. In his eagerness to secure a promise of Soviet assistance against Japan, he gave into Stalin's vague—but clearly expansionist—aims in Eastern Europe and Asia. Churchill was likely put off by the exuberance ad naïveté of his American friend, but there was nothing for him to do about it. Whatever the interpersonal dynamics, the Teheran Conference yielded some important results. The three leaders agreed to strike a final, decisive blow against Germany, and they pledged to support a new international peace-keeping organization to be called the United Nations.

The buildup of U.S. troops and supplies in Great Britain, already massive, was stepped up even further in the first five months of 1944. Then, on June 6, 1944—D-Day—the great invasion began. Under the leadership of General Eisenhower, some 110,000 American, British, and Canadian troops landed by air and sea on the Normandy coast of France. By the end of the month, more than 1 million men, 150,000 vehicles, and 500,000 tons of supplies were ashore. As the U.S. First Army pushed south and east out of Normandy, another Allied invasion force landed in mid-August on France's Mediterannean coast. Liberating armies entered Paris on August 25, moved on through Belgium, and crossed into Germany by September 11. Meanwhile, the Soviet army had begun a major new offensive on the eastern front. Advancing steadily westward, Russian tanks recaptured all Nazi-occupied lands and rolled beyond the original frontier by mid-September. The defeat of Hitler was clearly in sight.

Assessing War Policies

Even in times of war, American presidents are fair game for critics and second-guessers. National unity is itself a powerful weapon, but the democratic system defended by U.S. soldiers in World War II allows for reasonable expressions of disagreement with government policy. Franklin Roosevelt was not immune from such criticism. Although he did enjoy overwhelming popular support, several of his decisions came under attack. From Pearl Harbor to the defeat of Hitler, Roosevelt was blamed—sometimes fairly, sometimes not—for lapses in judgment and compassion.

First came the accusations that he had provoked an "incident" with Japan. Though this seems unlikely, the issue is yet being debated by historians. What can be concluded more safely, albeit with the benefit of hindsight, is that Roosevelt was both inflexible toward Japan in 1941 and naïve in regard to its militancy. Moreover, the Japanese surprise at Pearl Harbor was achieved with the help of poor communications between Washington and Hawaii in the days prior to the attack.

In the European theater, President Roosevelt was criticized for several policy decisions. The goal of unconditional surrender discouraged any anti-Hitler movement within Germany, some argued, because potential insurrectionists would have no prospects for an honorable settlement with the Allies. Also, the delay in establishing a "second front" angered some of Roosevelt's own generals, not to mention Stalin. Many historians have claimed that Russia's heavy load in the war caused so much resentment that it planted the seeds of the Cold War. Similarly, Roosevelt's generosity to Stalin at Teheran is frequently cited as the basis for the Soviet Union's postwar domination of Eastern Europe. Finally, the American president was criticized for the "strategic bombing" of civilian population centers in Germany. The city of Dresden is the most commonly cited example.

Five decades after World War II, however, the most nagging doubts about Roosevelt's war leadership have to do not with military planning or strategy but with civil liberties and basic human compassion. In one case he is accused of an egregious error of commission, in the other case of an unforgivable error of omission. In the former, he ordered the internment of thousands of Japanese-Americans on the West Coast. In the latter, he failed to take decisive action to save European Jews from extermination in Hitler's death camps.

After Pearl Harbor a clamor arose in California over the presence of Japanese on American soil. Politicians, members of the press, and private citizen groups expressed fear, suspicion, and a strong desire to "clean out the japs." In Washington federal officials began to feel the pressure. Finally, in early 1942, President Roosevelt ordered the detention of more than 110,000 Japanese-Americans, most of them U.S. citizens. Uprooted from their homes, businesses, and frequently each other, these California families were deported to detention camps hundreds of miles away. Amid the anger and fear during the months after Pearl Harbor, the action was widely accepted throughout the country. In later years, however, the American Civil Liberties Union (ACLU) called it "the worst single wholesale violation of civil rights of American citizens in our history."

Beginning in 1933 when Hitler came to power,

Roosevelt expressed concern over the plight of
Jews in Germany. As Hitler grew in power and as
his treatment of the Jews grew more tyrannical,
Roosevelt spoke out more forcefully against the
Nazi regime. American Jews favored early intervention in the war and backed their president
wholeheartedly. When the United States was finally drawn into the fighting, Roosevelt repeat-
edly warned the Nazis that they would be
punished for their crimes. By mid-1942 reliable
reports began reaching the president that Jews
were being murdered by the millions in Nazi
concentration camps. Rumors to that effect had
been circulating for some time, but they had
seemed too ghastly to be true. Now American
Jewish organizations appealed to Roosevelt to
take some action—any action. Opportunities existed to rescue small groups of Jews from certain
Axis-occupied countries, and Jewish leaders
pleaded with the White House and State Department. They implored Roosevelt to negotiate directly with Hitler for the release of Jews. Other
suggestions were to relax the Allied sea blockade
of Germany to allow in shipments of food and
medicine; to persuade neutral countries to open
their borders to escaping Jews; and to suspend
U.S. immigration quotas, allowing in more refu-
gees. The administration did nothing. Roosevelt

opposed any changes in the immigration law, re-sisted any promises of relief, refused to lift the blockade under any circumstances, and bristled at the thought of negotiating with Hitler on any-thing. The high moral standards that he had preached in the past were now strangely absent.

Whatever his failings as a strategist, diplomat, and moralist, Franklin Roosevelt's achievements during World War II cannot be overestimated. If he was slow in launching a second European front, adamant on the goal of unconditional sur-render, soft in his dealings with Stalin, harsh in his treatment of Japanese-Americans, and reluc-tant to help the Jews in Europe, it was all in the pursuit of final military victory (at least in his own mind). There were, in reality, two wars to be won—in Europe and the Pacific—and everything came together in the Oval Office. Roosevelt made the final decisions on overall military strategy, oversaw the greatest military buildup in history, and held together an unlikely diplomatic alliance. With buoyancy and faith, he made the hard deci-sions in the hardest of times. And perhaps most important, he inspired hope and confidence throughout the free world. More than any other figure in modern times, FDR projected faith in the survival of freedom and democracy.

8

The Fourth Term—Final Days

*"The only limit to our realization of tomorrow
will be our doubts of today"*

BY 1944 ROOSEVELT was tired and ailing. For more
than eleven years as chief executive, he had shoul-
dered the burdens of economic emergency, international upheaval, and, finally, world war. The
pressure was beginning to take its toll. At age 62,
the president was slowly losing his robust
strength and vast supply of energy. In early January a nagging case of the flu forced him to spend
a week at Hyde Park, and Eleanor expressed concern over her husband's state. In a letter to a
relative, she wrote: "FDR says he feels much
better but I don't think he longs to get back and
fight." In the spring Roosevelt suffered an inter-
mittent low fever and spent one month at the
South Carolina residence of Bernard Baruch, a
financier, statesman, and friend. Most dangerous
of all was a heart condition caused by hyperten-

sion. Fearing cardiac failure, a heart doctor was with the president at all times.

Franklin Roosevelt was also an increasingly lonely man. Even amid the hubbub of the White House, he missed many of the people who were closest to him. His four sons—James, Elliott, Franklin, Jr., and John—were all serving in the armed forces, and Eleanor was frequently away on tours of military bases, factories, hospitals, and service organizations. In war as in peacetime politics, the First Lady was away for long periods acting as the president's "legs and eyes." Others, including Sara in September 1941, had died. Louis Howe passed away in 1936. Secretaries Marvin McIntyre and Missy LeHand died in 1943 and 1944, respectively. And in late 1944, the president sent condolences to the wife of Reverend Endicott Peabody. "The whole tone of things is going to be a bit different from now on," he wrote, "for I have leaned on the Rector in all these many years far more than most people know."

Physically and perhaps emotionally, then, the time had come for Franklin Delano Roosevelt to leave the White House. But though he yearned for restful retirement at Hyde Park, he still saw a job to be done. The war against the Axis was still raging in both Europe and the Pacific, and the matter of global alignments in the postwar era still had to be resolved. In his unflagging sense of duty, he was determined to see the job done. In his stubborn personal pride and insatiable political ambition, he insisted on doing it himself. By the summer of 1944 he had decided to set aside personal discomfort and seek a fourth term as president of the United States. One week before the party's July convention, Roosevelt stated his intention in a note to the Democratic national chairman. "All that is in me cries out to go back to my home on the Hudson River," he wrote, "but we of this generation chance to live in a day and hour when our Nation has been attacked, and when its future existence and the future existence of our chosen method of government are at stake."

There was little opposition to Roosevelt's renomination. With his health in obvious decline, however, attention focused on the vice-presidency. If the president was unable to complete his term of office, was Vice-President Wallace a good replacement? Many in the party felt he was too liberal and too temperamental to be chief executive. His being on the ticket might hurt Roosevelt's chances in the election. Several of the president's advisers recommended that Wallace be dropped and Harry S. Truman, a senator from Missouri, be taken on as a running mate. The president consented.

From the outset, Roosevelt's announced intention was to stay off the campaign trail. With the war effort in its critical states, he felt he should not be away from Washington. "In these days of tragic sorrow," he said, "I do not consider it fitting." Roosevelt, the most seasoned of political campaigners, also realized that the public might be alarmed by his unhealthy appearance. One visitor to the White House wrote the following description in his diary: "I was terrified when I saw his face. I felt certain he was going to die. . . . I could not get over the ravaged expression of his face. It was gray, gaunt, and sagging, and the muscles controlling the lips seemed to have lost part of their function."

The Republicans, meanwhile, chose another New York governor, Thomas E. Dewey, as their nominee for the presidency. The fourth different candidate the GOP had put up against Roosevelt, Dewey, was a youthful and exuberant campaigner, with a vibrant speaking style that attracted large crowds at every stop. Wall Street still harbored a deep hatred of "That Man in the White House," and Dewey cultivated public resentment of the president's enormous power. As Dewey's popularity grew, Roosevelt realized that he would have to alter his strategy. Still resisting a formal campaign, he began taking long "nonpartisan" inspection tours of military facilities across the country. Along the way, he stopped at hundreds of cities and towns to wave to crowds, shake hands, and kiss babies. Then, in the final weeks before the election, the president made several dramatic appearances to remind the voters of his vitality and charm.

On one such occasion in late September, Roosevelt gave one of the most endearing and most effective speeches in the annals of American politics. In remarks broadcast by radio from a Teamsters' Union convention in Washington, Roosevelt served notice that he could still fight his political battles with a cutting wit. Days earlier, a newspaper column alleged that FDR had sent a Navy destroyer to retrieve his dog, Fala, from the Aleutian Islands, where he had been left behind on a presidential visit to Alaska. Roosevelt put on a look of mock sorrow as he faced the audience of Teamsters. ''These Republican leaders have not been content with attacks on me, on my wife, or on my sons,'' he said in all seriousness. ''No, not content with that, they now include my little dog, Fala. Well, of course I don't resent attacks, and my family doesn't resent attacks, but Fala *does* resent them.'' The reason? Money. Fala was outraged at the expense of sending a destroyer to fetch him. ''Being a Scottie,'' the president smiled, ''his Scotch soul was furious. He has not been the same dog since!'' The audience exploded.

Roosevelt's finishing campaign kick included a daylong tour of New York City in late October. To demonstrate his physical stamina, he sat in the back of an open touring car wearing just an old hat and boat cloak in a drenching rainstorm. His doctors were not pleased, but at least one witness noticed that, back on the campaign stump, FDR has "improved visibly in strength and resilience." The day before the election, Roosevelt again sat in the back of an open car, this time for a "sentimental journey" through the Hudson River Valley. It was thirty-four years since he had campaigned there for his first public office.

The 1944 election proved to be the closest of Roosevelt's four tries for the presidency, but he still won comfortably. The margin of victory was 432 to 99 in the electoral college and 25,602,505 to Dewey's 22,006,278 in the popular vote. On January 20, 1945, the oath of office was administered at the White House instead of the Capitol to save energy and money. James Roosevelt and a Marine guard lifted the helpless president to the lectern for a short and labored inaugural address.

Yalta

In early 1945 the war was reaching a climax on both fronts. With Nazi Germany on its last legs and Japanese forces giving ground fast, the terms

In February 1945, the Big Three (Churchill, FDR, and Stalin) met at Yalta to discuss plans for the postwar world. Their decisions and agreements have had a lasting effect on international relations.

of peace were becoming an urgent matter for the Allied leaders. In his inaugural speech, President Roosevelt dedicated himself to ''a just and honorable peace, a durable peace.'' He vowed to pursue it doggedly and in good faith. ''We can gain no lasting peace,'' he proclaimed, ''if we approach it with suspicion and mistrust—or with fear.'' It was in this spirit that he set sail three days later for a meeting with Churchill and Stalin at Yalta, in the Crimea.

Roosevelt and his staff arrived at Yalta on February 4. Chief among his advisers was Secretary of State Edward J. Stettinius, Jr., who had replaced the retired Cordell Hull. Winston Churchill found his American friend hollow-eyed and frail, but for the weeklong conference FDR was as buoyant and lighthearted as ever. In later years it was alleged that Stalin took advantage of a sick U.S. president, but Roosevelt's judgment was in no way altered by ill health. One of his main objectives at the conference was to fix a date for Soviet entrance into the war against Japan. As always, he was most concerned with solving the immediate problem at hand—in this case, winning the war. Stalin, however, was more interested in securing territory in the postwar era. None of the parties at Yalta had everything go his way. In a week of hard bargaining, compromises were reached on a broad range of issues.

Many of the agreements reached at Yalta were kept secret until after the war was over. For the time being, Roosevelt did secure a commitment from Stalin to enter the fighting in the Pacific by a specific date. In return, the Soviet Union was promised territories in the Far East. The political status of Eastern Europe remained ambiguous, but the Yalta agreement made it easy for the USSR to take control. The Soviet sphere of influence in the postwar era did have its roots in Yalta, and Roosevelt has been blamed for not protecting against Stalin's expansionist ambitions.

Other agreements reached in the Crimea would affect international relations for decades to come. After the war, Germany was to be divided into U.S., French, British, and Soviet zones, all governed by an Allied Control Commission. The capital city of Berlin, located within the Soviet zone, was similarly divided into four sectors. Differences between the USSR and the Western Allies eventually led to the formation of East Germany in 1949 and the construction of the Berlin Wall in 1961. According to the Yalta accords, reparations from Germany would be divided equally among the four Allied powers. German assets would be confiscated and its industrial plants dismantled. A special international court was to be established to exact justice for Nazi war crimes. And, of deep importance to President Roosevelt, there was a meeting of the minds on the proposed United Nations organization. A formula was agreed upon for voting in the Security Council, and a conference to draft the United Nations Charter was scheduled for late April in San Francisco.

For several years, Roosevelt and the State Department had been heavily promoting the cause of a new international peace-keeping organization. Having learned his lesson from President Wilson's handling of the League of Nations concept, Roosevelt sought congressional support in planning the organization. In 1943 Secretary of State Hull carried the idea to Moscow, where the British, Soviet and Chinese governments agreed on a prospective world body "based on the principle of the sovereign equality of all peace-loving states, and open to membership by all such states, large and small." More detailed plans were made at the Dumbarton Oaks Conference near Washington from August 21 to October 7, 1944. With the question of the Security Council resolved at Yalta, all that needed to be worked out was the wording of the formal charter.

Promised Land and Home on the Hudson

On March 1, 1945, two days after his return to Washington, Roosevelt appeared before Congress to report on the Yalta talks and to ask support for the San Francisco Conference. A standing ovation greeted the president as he was wheeled to the front of the chamber. When he was lifted from his wheelchair and seated before a small table below the rostrum, a hush fell over the audience. His face was thin and pale, his voice weak and flat.

"I hope you will pardon me for the unusual posture of sitting down during the presentation of what I want to say," he began, "but I know you will realize it makes it a lot easier for me in not having to carry about ten pounds of steel around the bottom of my legs; and also because I have just completed a 14,000-mile trip." As he stumbled through a long and somewhat rambling speech, many in the audience feared it was the last time they would ever see him.

The president's physician ordered "a period of total rest," and on March 29 Roosevelt left Washington for the Little White House at Warm Springs. After a few days of sun and relaxation, color returned to his face and his spirits improved. His only major worry was Stalin, whose motives were becoming increasingly obvious. Otherwise, the promised land of peace seemed just over the horizon. Germany was beaten, Japan was on the ropes, and American scientists were nearing completion of their secret work on an atomic bomb. On April 30 Hitler would commit suicide. On May 8 victory would be declared in Europe. And on August 14, after atomic bombs had destroyed two major cities, the Japanese would surrender. For Franklin Roosevelt, however, the end would come before any of this could happen.

On Thursday morning, April 12, 1945, the president read the newspaper and worked on his stamp collection in the sun-filled living room of his Georgia retreat. With him at Warm Springs were his doctor, a secretary, two cousins, and Lucy Rutherford—the former Lucy Mercer. After the death of her husband several years before, Lucy had been invited to the White House for frequent dinners with the president. Eleanor was never present, and she did not learn of the renewed liaison until after her husband's death.

Lucy had commissioned a portrait of the president, and the artist arrived some time around noon. Roosevelt put on a dark blue suit and a Harvard-red tie, and settled into a leather chair near the fireplace. As the artist worked, the president signed some documents. All of a sudden he put his hand to his temple and groaned, "I have a terrific headache." He slumped sideways, and four hours later he was dead of a massive cerebral hemorrhage—a large broken blood vessel in the brain.

Eleanor arrived in Warm Springs the next morning and made arrangements to take her husband home. The coffin was loaded on a funeral train, and tearful crowds gathered along the route to wave good-bye. After a funeral procession and short ceremony in Washington, the body was

During a visit to Warm Springs, Georgia, on April 12, 1945, FDR died at age 63. His body was sent by train to Washington, D.C. for the funeral procession.

transported to Hyde Park, where it was buried in the Rose Garden.

On the afternoon before his death, Roosevelt had drafted a short speech to commemorate Jefferson Day on April 13. The speech was to be broadcast by radio to 350 Jefferson Day dinners around the country. Though he never got to deliver the speech, it was fitting that his last public address would honor the founding father most deeply committed to the will of the common people. Roosevelt began his speech by paying tribute to the "living memory of Thomas Jefferson." He ended it with a call for lasting peace and freedom. "The only limit to our realization of tomorrow," he said, "will be our doubts of today. Let us move forward with strong and active faith."

For subsequent generations of Americans, that faith would be the "living memory" of Franklin Delano Roosevelt. The "realization of tomorrow" would bear his unmistakable imprint.

9

The Man and His Legacy

*"The fate of America cannot depend
on any one man. The greatness of
America is grounded in principles
and not on any single personality"*

In JANUARY 1982, the United States celebrated the
100th birthday of Franklin Delano Roosevelt. The
centennial was officially observed in twelve states
and twenty major cities. Federal observances in
Washington, D.C., included six exhibitions of
Roosevelt memorabilia, the issuing of a new FDR
stamp, and a special joint session of Congress to
honor the nation's only four-term president.
Thirty-seven years after his passing, however,
Roosevelt was still a controversial figure. The centennial itself was a small, modestly financed affair
compared with commemorations for other American leaders. The $200,000 spent by the govern-
ment, for example, paled in comparison with the
$7 million spent on the Herbert Hoover centennial

in 1974. Conspicuously absent from most of the FDR festivities was President Ronald Reagan, who turned down invitations to the various functions. And amid all the nostalgia and high praise from carriers of the Roosevelt flame, the magazine of the Republican National Committee, *Source*, labeled FDR "the great chiseler."

The ironies and contradictions of the Roosevelt centennial were a fitting tribute to the thirty-second president. If nothing else, they underscored the strong influence that Franklin Roosevelt still has on American public life. His lasting impact on voting patterns and the Democratic party were evidenced by the noncelebratory mood of the Republican administration. The economic and social reforms begun during the New Deal were still very much at issue when President Reagan delivered his State of the Union message four days before Roosevelt's 100th birthday. By promising to limit government spending, cut federal aid programs, eliminate regulatory controls, and reduce the overall role of government, Reagan was taking on the ghost of FDR. Finally, the period in American history that became known as the Age of Roosevelt was itself fraught with irony and contradiction.

In one of this last campaign speeches before the 1932 election, the Democratic candidate who had been winning votes with his dynamic spirit and irrepressible charm spoke to a gathering in New York City about the job of president. "The fate of America," Roosevelt insisted, "cannot depend on any one man. The greatness of America is grounded in principles and not on any single personality."

The irony of his words would not be known for a good many years. For as the Age of Roosevelt recedes in history, it has become increasingly clear that the life of the nation and the spirit of its people were determined in great measure by the personality of a single man. The successes and failures of FDR's presidency mirrored the strengths and weaknesses of his temperament. His optimism, fortitude, and ability to inspire confidence were more valuable in combating poverty and Nazi aggression than any economic policy or military strategy. His arrogance and lust for power expanded presidential authority and the role of government to an unprecedented level. His sympathy for the poor and underprivileged began a revolution in economic and social reform. He was a self-proclaimed champion of civil rights who did little to help American blacks and who jailed thousands of Japanese-Americans on the grounds of race alone. He was an old-fashioned moralist who refused even to denounce the death

Roosevelt's personality—his fortitude, confidence, and jaunty optimism—helped the nation survive its two greatest crises of the 20th century: the Great Depression and World War II.

camps and gas chambers of Hitler's Germany. He was a passionate defender of democracy who sought to "pack" the Supreme Court with his own men and who deceived the American people about U.S. neutrality prior to World War II. The contradictions of the time reflected the impulsiveness, flexibility, and often conflicting roles of its leader.

In the same way that contemporaries of Roosevelt argued about the effectiveness and propriety of his actions, so historians continue to debate the meaning and value of his presidency. But even as the controversy persists, the record ultimately must speak for itself. If it is contradictory and sometimes even mystifying, the reason is Roosevelt himself. As one commentator has written: "Let the historians disagree; after all, it was personality." For FDR more than for any other American president, the man was the measure of his accomplishments and the accomplishments the measure of the man. The only conclusion that can be drawn with any certainty is that Franklin Roosevelt had a deep and lasting impact on life in America—indeed, the world. For better, for worse, and for just the way things are, his influence is immeasurable.

The New Deal and Beyond

After a visit by Franklin Roosevelt in 1932, retired Supreme Court Justice Oliver Wendell Holmes made a keen assessment of the up-and-coming candidate. "A second-class intellect," the sage determined, "but a first-class temperament!" Roosevelt had a practical mind that could range over a whole series of problems, analyze possible solutions, and recognize the merits in each. He was not, however, a deep or original thinker. A man of action, he resisted any strict philosophy and had little patience for ideological debate. "During all the time I was associated with him," said one member of the Brain Trust, "I never knew him to read a serious book." At the same time, he was an idealist and reformer, a bold experimenter, a cheerful optimist, an actor and showman, and a strong leader with an unfailing drive to succeed.

Those qualities were no more evident than in his efforts to end the Great Depression. "At the heart of the New Deal," according to historian Richard Hofstadter, "was not a philosophy but a temperament." Other than a commitment to the Forgotten Man, a hatred of big business, and a belief in the reconstructive power of government, the New Deal was guided by no firm ideology. With a promise for "action, and action now," Roosevelt engineered a sweeping program of re-covery and reform. He surrounded himself with advisers of varied backgrounds and ideas, and he was willing to try anything. It was a bold, freewheeling, almost desperate experiment in government action. Its random, hodgepodge character was both its triumph and its failing. The steadfast spirit, social vision, and political skill of Franklin Roosevelt were its backbone.

The impact of the New Deal is still felt in everyday life throughout the United States. Many of the roads, bridges, tunnels, dams, power plants, hospitals, schools, and libraries built by the PWA, WPA, TVA, and other New Deal agencies continue to be used. There are works of art, irrigation canals and sewage systems, guidebooks and histories, national monuments, parks, playgrounds, ball fields, and hiking trails. Popular artists and prizewinning writers were supported in their early years by federal programs. From the Grand Coulee Dam to Jackson Pollock murals, the New Deal brought lasting changes to the physical and cultural landscape of America.

Of an equally enduring character were the institutions created by Roosevelt to prevent the occurrence of another Great Depression. Among the New Deal innovations still in effect are regulation of the stock, bond, and securities markets; price controls on agricultural products; stimulations for the housing industry; and federal insurance on bank deposits. These have ensured that an economic collapse like that of 1929 will not occur again.

Closely tied in with these economic reform measures are social programs and institutions to promote the well-being of all Americans. Social security, unemployment insurance, the progressive income tax, minimum wages, maximum work hours, and mandatory retirement pensions were just the beginning of a major new trend in the American system. The new outlook has been called a variety of things, including "social democracy" and "state capitalism." What it amounts to, however, is the assumption of greater responsibility by the federal government for the economic and social well-being of the nation. With the New Deal, Washington began supporting the private sector, regulating business, and caring for the poor to a far greater degree than ever before in American history.

Rather than dismantle New Deal agencies, subsequent presidents have continued the trend toward increased government authority. In addition to exploring new areas of federal participation, they have funded existing institutions with growing generosity. Agencies created during the 1930s remain a powerful force in American government. Surviving New Deal institutions include the Civil Aeronautics Board (CAB), Commodity Credit Corporation (CCC), Export-Import Bank (EIB), Farm Credit Administration (FCA), Federal Communications Commission (FCC), Federal Deposit Insurance Corporation (FDIC), Federal Housing Administration (FHA), Federal Savings and Loan Insurance Corporation (FSLIC), National Labor Relations Board (NLRB), Rural Electrification Administration (REA), Securities and Exchange Commission (SEC), Social Security Administration (SSA), and Tennessee Valley Authority (TVA).

Ronald Reagan was the first American president firmly to resist the trend begun by the New Deal. Big Government, he maintained, has become a monster. Regulations have become burdensome to private industry and damaging to the economy. Excessively generous aid programs have created a welfare state and contributed to an enormous national debt. Labor demands too much, and the federal bureaucracy has grown unwieldy. Not even President Reagan could hold Franklin Roosevelt entirely to blame, of course, but continued heavy spending by the government does create dangers. And even though Roosevelt is not alive to argue his case, the centrality of the entire issue in American life today is testimony to the lasting impact of the New Deal. Beyond that, there is evidence that Roosevelt was at least partly correct. Even with all his budget restrictions and cutbacks in federal aid, President Reagan was reluctant to tamper with such New Deal institutions as social security, farm price supports, or the Tennessee Valley Authority.

Whatever its long-term consequences, the New Deal did accomplish its primary objective— relieving the effects of the Great Depression. When Franklin Roosevelt came to office, the entire economic system was in jeopardy. America was on its knees. And while his programs never did bring a complete cure, they did avert catastrophe.

The Postwar World

World War II and the events leading up to it tested Roosevelt's leadership as even the Great Depression had not done. His handling of the war effort brought into even sharper focus the strengths and weaknesses of his leadership. He was caught sleeping by the attack on Pearl Harbor. He hesitated on the invasion of Europe. His morality failed him in dealing with Japanese-Americans at home and Jews in Europe. He deceitfully compromised U.S. neutrality in the two years before war was declared. And he grabbed power with little regard for the system of checks and balances among the three branches of government. But whatever his failings, FDR must be regarded as a great war president by the mere fact that he led the Allies to victory. Whatever his tactics and whatever his mistakes, he was, in the end, "Dr. Win-the-War." He rose to the occasion, and the outcome was never in doubt. Ever an inspirer of confidence, he made the nation feel invincible. His prewar tactics may have been deceitful, but they proved correct and necessary in the face of Hitler's very real threat. His failures are ultimately negligible in comparison with the single achievement of winning the war. His legacy as a war president is nothing less than the survival of democracy.

In preparations for peace as in the conduct of war, Roosevelt was both a pragmatist and a visionary. He had the imagination and the nerve to launch the uncertain atomic bomb project, which ultimately saved lives by bringing the war to a quick end. At the same time, he realized that such a weapon would open a whole new era in world affairs, one that would require new institutions of peace and a new spirit of global cooperation. If Allied war strategy alienated Stalin, and if Roosevelt gave in to the Soviet leader at Yalta, it was for the immediate purpose of bringing the war to a successful conclusion. Many historians have blamed FDR for taking a short-term view of the conflict and not looking far enough ahead to the political aftermath. Although the seeds of the cold war were indeed sown during World War II, the criticisms of Roosevelt are not entirely fair. He did not live to cultivate his friendship with Stalin or, if necessary, take a hard line against Soviet expansion in Eastern Europe. Moreover, Roosevelt had been looking toward the postwar world since before the United States even entered the fighting. As early as July 1940 he called for a world founded on his so-called Four Freedoms: freedom of speech, freedom of religion, freedom from want, and freedom from fear of aggression. Nor were Roosevelt's efforts to secure peace in the postwar era totally without result. His great gift in that regard was the United Nations, of which he was the chief architect and spiritual father.

Politics and the Presidency

As a political leader, Roosevelt was unsurpassed in jockeying for power and winning support for his views. His second four years in office were largely a failure, but his skill as a politician still enabled him to win an unprecedented third term as president. In style as well as in achievement, his tenure in the White House has had a long-lasting effect on voting alignments, the office of the presidency, and the American political process in general.

FDR's political strategy, especially during the New Deal, frequently has been characterized as "broker leadership." Without any ideological commitments, he was able to attract a wide range of powerful constituencies into his camp. As a broker of power, he traded, compromised, promised, cajoled, arm-twisted, wheeled, dealed, and otherwise mediated among all potential members of a Grand Coalition. The random and ill-assorted programs of the New Deal manifested Roosevelt's effort to win over as many economic blocs and pressure groups as he could. There was, in short, something for everyone—except big business and the wealthy class. By dealing power in exchange for support and by remaining flexible in day-to-day policy making, Roosevelt forged a powerful political alliance. And though such power brokering is a pragmatic strategy usually intended to bring short-term political gains, Roosevelt's Democratic coalition remains relatively intact today. Party strength is still founded on farmers, blue-collar workers, minorities, Catholics, Jews, city bosses, labor, the left, and the South. That constellation of support has been the making or breaking of every Democratic presidential candidate since FDR. Any major breakdown spells defeat on election day.

There have been four Democratic presidents since FDR: Harry Truman, John F. Kennedy, Lyndon Johnson, and Jimmy Carter. Truman was his chosen successor. Kennedy was the son of his ambassador to Great Britain. And Lyndon Johnson was his pet congressman in the late 1930s; when LBJ became president in 1963, he declared that Roosevelt would be his model. Truman's "Fair Deal," Kennedy's "New Frontier," and Johnson's "Great Society" were all domestic aid programs in the tradition of Roosevelt's New Deal. Even his Republican successors—Dwight Eisenhower, Richard Nixon, Gerald Ford, and Ronald Reagan—have acknowledged Roosevelt's influence to some degree.

FDR's leadership during the Great Depression and World War II has established him—rightly or wrongly—as the standard by which American presidents are judged. The public has come to expect in its leaders the same qualities that FDR showed in times of extreme crisis. However, Roosevelt's heritage is not one of greatness alone. His appetite for power and willingness to deceive set dangerous precedents, which Congress has been forced to curb. Of particular concern has been the expansion of presidential war power. Roosevelt's deception of the people and disregard of Congress were models that several presidents followed during the Vietnam era.

Finally, Roosevelt's use of the media added a whole new dimension to the American political process. Early in his career, he recognized the value of the radio and the press in showcasing his personal charm and in making his ideas known to the public. His twenty-eight Fireside Chats enabled him to go over the head of Congress to make his appeals directly to the people. In the depths of the Depression and at the height of tension in World War II, the radio was invaluable in rallying the American people. In subsequent decades, the broadcast media established a critical link between the president and the public. Politics was brought out of smoky back rooms and into the living room.

Roosevelt's use of the print media had similar political advantages. The press conference allowed him to exert influence on newspaper presentation of critical issues. By highlighting certain aspects of his policy and downplaying others, he could guide public debate. By making the press conference a free and open exchange with reporters, he could also find out what problems were on people's minds and to what extent he was succeeding or failing in a given area. And beyond his 998 press conferences, Roosevelt also employed clever tactics to use newspapers as a feedback device, or sounding board. With characteristic guile, he would leak information or plant rumors just to find out the public's response. Roosevelt was not always on the best terms with the press, but he used it to full advantage. One result was a heavy increase in the amount of news emanating from Washington. The wire services increased their output of information several-fold, and the public knew what was going on in greater detail. This was a circumstance with which all future presidents would have to contend. The press could be a great boon for a chief executive, but it also put the office under closer scrutiny.

Franklin Delano Roosevelt was, in short, a man of great contradiction whose impact on life in America has been equaled by few other presidents. Born into patrician wealth, his dedication to the poor and forgotten made him a ''traitor to his class.'' He was lighthearted and personable, but even those closest to him did not know him well. He was stubborn and self-reliant, but his character was deeply influenced by others: the dynamism and ambition of Cousin Ted, the idealism and civic duty of Endicott Peabody, the wiliness of Louis Howe, the high-society airs of Sara, and the humanitarianism of Eleanor. His physical

handicap made him a stronger man, and his fortitude made him an example to others. He was
moral and high-minded, but he was unfaithful to
his wife and planned "dirty tricks" against political adversaries.

Roosevelt was accused time and again of being
a dictator, but his instincts and his ultimate purpose were too purely democratic for the label to
fit. Good fortune made him the most attractive
candidate when the opportunity for greatness
was his for the taking. A second opportunity presented itself when his political standing was at its
lowest. In both cases, his unique style of leadership and distinctive personal qualities were well
suited to the tasks at hand. "If ever the right man
came to occupy the office at the right time," said
historian Heinz Eulau, "Franklin D. Roosevelt
was that man."

For Further Reading

Few figures in modern history have been written about more extensively than Franklin Delano Roosevelt. Many leading historians have focused their attention on him, and literally hundreds of books and articles have been written about his life, his times, and his accomplishments. For the interested reader, there is a rich literature to sample.

The most thorough and comprehensive works are those by Arthur M. Schlesinger, Jr., and Frank Freidel. Schlesinger's *The Age of Roosevelt* is a projected six-volume history of which three volumes have thus far appeared: *The Crisis of the Old Order, 1919–1933; The Coming of the New Deal;* and *The Politics of Upheaval.* Freidel's multi-volume biography, also incomplete as yet, includes *Franklin D. Roosevelt: The Apprenticeship; Franklin D. Roosevelt: The Ordeal; Franklin D. Roosevelt: The Triumph;* and *Franklin D. Roosevelt: Launching the New Deal.*

Important single-volume works are James MacGregor Burns' *Roosevelt: The Lion and the Fox,* a "political biography," and *Roosevelt: The Soldier of Freedom,* which focuses on FDR during the war years. For younger readers, *FDR* by Finis Farr and *Franklin D. Roosevelt—Portrait of a Great Man* by

Gerald W. Johnson are informative and highly readable. For both young and old, Joseph Alsop's *FDR: A Centenary Remembrance* provides lively reading and a wealth of photographs.

In addition to these general biographies, there are numerous books and articles devoted to specific areas of interest. Perhaps most abundant are those pertaining to the New Deal and the Depression. William E. Leuchtenberg's *Franklin D. Roosevelt and the New Deal* is a detailed historical account. An interesting theoretical approach is taken by Arthur A. Kekirch, Jr., in *Ideologies and Utopias: The Impact of the New Deal on American Thought*. Magazine articles that appeared during the FDR centennial in 1982 are most useful in sorting out Roosevelt's New Deal and its impact. *The Wilson Quarterly* (Spring 1982) devotes a whole section to the subject: "Prelude" by Alan Brinkley, "The New Deal Reconsidered" by Bradford A. Lee, and "The Legacy of FDR" by William E. Leuchtenberg. Similar treatment is given in "F.D.R.'s Disputed Legacy," *Time*, February 1, 1982.

Eleanor and Franklin, a biography of Eleanor Roosevelt, by Joseph Lash gives much background on Franklin and their relationship. *The Autobiography of Eleanor Roosevelt* and *Eleanor Roosevelt* by Sharon Whitney tell the story of the "First Lady of the World."

Index